S0-DYV-757

SINGLES, SEX & MARRIAGE

Books By Herbert J. Miles

The Dating Game

Sexual Understanding before Marriage

Sexual Happiness in Marriage

HERBERT J. MILES

SINGLES, SEX & MARRIAGE

WORD BOOKS
PUBLISHER
WACO, TEXAS
A DIVISION OF
WORD, INCORPORATED

SINGLES, SEX AND MARRIAGE

Library of Congress Cataloging in Publication Data

Miles, Herbert Jackson, 1907–
Singles, sex, and marriage.

Bibliography: p.
1. Single people. 2. Single people—Religious life.
3. Sex. 4. Marriage. I. Title.
HQ800.M47 1983 306.7'3'0880652 83-6736
ISBN 0-8499-0361-0

Printed in the United States of America

Dedicated
to
Fern Harrington Miles
my wife
a single missionary to the Chinese
in the Orient
for thirty-five years

Contents

Preface

The grave and critical sexual disorder of our time and the over-emphasis on personal freedom have gradually undermined, demoralized, and corrupted the institution of marriage and have placed a halo over singleness. This trend is nationwide and even worldwide. So excessive and distorted is this abrupt moral twist and wrench that the very foundations of the kingdom of God, and, as a result, the social order, are threatened. I believe this rash change in the relationships of male and female demands a biblical reinterpretation of the nature of love and marriage in terms of personal relationships and a consequent reorientation of our attitudes and ideas concerning singles, sex, and marriage. Needed is a clearer definition of what God intended male and female to be, i.e., a clear description of male uniqueness and female uniqueness. We need to know how this uniqueness of the two sexes cooperates in the biblical one-flesh union. In a word, we need to know what this union is all about, and certainly we need Christian guidelines to help singles handle sexuality before marriage.

I hope to help my single readers study their present blueprint concerning singleness and marriage, by analyzing the following: (1) where are you? (2) how did you get there? and (3) where will your present plans take you? You need to thoroughly think through where you believe God wants you to go, and how your attitudes about singleness and marriage square with biblical teachings.

Singles, Sex, and Marriage is a Christian view of singleness and marriage, of true "maleness" and true "femaleness."

I gratefully acknowledge my indebtedness to dozens of people who have made contributions to the writing of this volume. I am grateful to college professors Jan Marie A. Strong (sociology), Susan H. Ambler (sociology), and John Burton (physics) for assisting me in our never-married singles research. I am deeply indebted to the following never-married singles who evaluated the manuscript and made countless suggestions during fourteen two-hour seminar sessions: Dorothy Barkley; Cathy Damron; Bruce Davenport; Donna Davenport; Wayne Earley; Kathy Fitzgerald; Angie France; Ken Frazier; Ricke Hester; Doug Lewis; Donna Mitchell; Karen Montgomery; Dianne Robinette; and Wayne Strong, a church leader of singles.

I am especially grateful to Fern Harrington Miles, a single adult for forty years, who became my wife after I had experienced singleness in widowhood. She was my consultant and constant companion during the writing of the manuscript. I want to express my personal thanks to Sharon Krause, single and a college professor of English, who read the entire manuscript and made many valuable suggestions. I am exceedingly grateful to my secretary, Bonnie Vanaman, a college junior, who typed the manuscript from the first draft through its various stages to its final form.

HERBERT J. MILES

Carson-Newman College
Jefferson City, TN 37760

PART I

The Divine Plans for Male and Female

1

When You Meet a Fact in the Road, Face It

As a ten-year-old farm boy, I had an experience that taught me a valuable lesson. While visiting Robert, a neighborhood playmate, I overheard my friend's father and a neighbor telling stories about snakes. Sitting out in the yard under a shade tree near the family's outdoor cellar, they told stories about a snake that would wrap itself around its prey and squeeze it to death, a joint snake that would break into several pieces under enemy attack, and a hoop snake that would roll after an enemy, killing that enemy by a nail attached to its tail. These stories filled my boyish imagination with fear about snakes.

During the next week I was walking home from school with Jim, age fourteen, when we suddenly came upon a snake about five feet long, lying in the middle of the road. Remembering the snake stories, I panicked. Turning around, I quickly climbed a high embankment and scaled a woven wire fence with three strands of barbed wire on top. Ready to take off for parts unknown, I turned to check on Jim's safety. He was beating the snake with a large stick he had picked up by the side of the road. He called to me, "Come on back, I've killed the snake!"

In later years I learned that the neighbor's cellar contained a barrel of elderberry wine. The men had imbibed too freely—hence their stimulated imagination which produced the snake stories.

Also, I learned that snakes are our friends, and most of them are quite harmless.

From that childhood experience, I learned a significant truth—when you meet a fact in the road, face it. Don't be afraid of facts. Too often when problems arise, in our insecurity and fear, we panic, turn, and run. What we need to do is turn toward the facts involved, examine them, study them, if necessary do battle with them, and conquer them. Like snakes, most facts are our friends. When understood and experienced in the context of Christian love, facts can promote our welfare and happiness. This book is planned to help those journeying through singleness toward marriage come to grips with the facts of human sexuality.

Who are the singles? In addition to young adults, they are the never-married older men and women, the widows, the widowers, the separated, or the divorced. There are approximately fifty-three million of them in our society—almost one-fourth of our population. They are God's creation, made in his image. They live and breathe and work and eat and sleep like all other people. They have emotional and physical needs, ambitions, dreams, and are concerned about duty, responsibility, and altruistic service like the rest of the population. Which is the most neglected group in America? Blacks? Hispanics? Could it be singles?

In the past decade, many good books have been published that deal with the problems of the widowed and/or the divorced. But those who have never married have received very little attention. The main thrust of this book is toward those who have never married. However, much of what we have to say will be positive and meaningful to the widowed and divorced since they share many of the same needs.

In creating mankind in his image, God created them "male and female" (Gen. 1:27). This verse contains the first reference to sex in the Bible. The Scriptures go on to say that God created sex to be experienced in the marriage relationship (Gen. 2:24). This theme is emphasized and stressed in the Scriptures, especially in the teachings of Jesus, Paul, and the other apostles. Since this is true, *why then a book on "singles, sex, and marriage"?*

First, it is a fact that God created males with a strong sexual drive and females with a strong sexual need. This drive and this need are the same for all, a fact that presents singles with a major problem: *How are they to manage and control these sexual drives and needs in singleness and live within Christian moral guidelines?*

Second, in the past, evangelicals have published good books giving details about how married couples should manage and control their sexual needs.[1] But evangelicals have not published similar books zeroing in on the sexual problems of the unmarried. In the last decade, much good material has been written on singleness. But most of it has dealt in general on how to handle the problems of social interaction in a society of married couples. Some of these books have one chapter on singles and sex.[2]

Third, our sinful culture, guided by the relativism of humanism and of situation ethics, encourages and promotes all kinds of sexual permissiveness. Some of its guidelines are "sex is normal between consenting adults," and "if it feels good, it must be right." The conflict between our Christian guidelines and our cultural guidelines leaves many singles confused.

Finally, some are calling for specific help in the form of literature that comes to grips with their sexual needs and their concern for a good marriage. The following two letters to Susan Deitz, syndicated columnist, tell the story of the deep inner feelings and heartaches rarely expressed openly by many never-marrieds:

> Dear Susan: I am amazed and sometimes angered at the way people who are married view those of us who aren't. Many did not choose lifelong singleness; a lifetime of loneliness and frustration for want of loving and being loved often lies behind our façade. How many people know what others are really feeling inside, regardless of what they say or how they act? Doesn't it occur to anyone that the right person may have died, or that, for a multitude of other reasons, things just haven't worked out for some people?
>
> Our segment of the population is made up of the forgotten people. The professionals show great concern for the divorced, the married,

the widowed, but they seem to have no insight into the never-marrieds' problems.[3]

Dear Susan: We single people need support sometimes and to find out that we are not out there alone. Your column helps. I'm aware of advice books on broken marriages, loss of spouse, and so on, but are there any books for single people with high expectations and morals?[4]

These letters are only the tip of the iceberg. Thousands of other never-marrieds have the same heart-hunger for the blessings of marriage but have lacked the courage to write a letter to a columnist or to speak out publicly. We propose to speak in their behalf. (See Appendix I, "Reflections on Singleness.")

This book is planned to help the thousands of singles, male and female, who have high expectations and high morals, and who need support. I am confident they are open to and will welcome suggestions on *how to cope with sex during singleness and how to plan toward a good marriage*.

People are asking: What does the Bible say about marriage? About singleness? What are singles supposed to do with their sex drive? What are acceptable ways in God's sight to meet our sexual needs? What can we do in order to meet eligible prospects and realize a good marriage? We propose to help our readers think through these questions.

Second to their need for God, sexual need poses one of the most difficult problems facing single people. Sexual need, however, involves more than the physical act of sex.

Sexual need has many facets—the need for companionship, the need of a sense of self-worth, the need to love and be loved, the need to be self-giving, the need for physical intimacy, and the need to meet maternal and paternal instincts. Most of these needs can be broken down and partially met in various appropriate ways. By using creative ingenuity in one's vocation, there is ample opportunity for self-giving and self-worth. By serving others in unselfish ways, one can love and feel loved. Through contacts with the children of relatives, the church, and community, singles can have some of the joys of parenthood without the responsibility.[5]

Meeting the need for sexual intimacy is probably our most baffling problem. The deep hunger for that one special person of the opposite sex to love in that special way according to God's creative plan causes us much frustration and heartache. Thus I propose to zero in upon two needs: (1) the problem of managing and controlling sexual drives during the various experiences of singleness, and (2) the process of meeting an acceptable marriage prospect and building a wise and productive marriage.

2

God, Sex, and You

To help us face reality about our future as related to our sexuality and marriage, let us make a study of the purpose of human sexuality as reflected in biblical revelation. After creating the heavens and earth, light and darkness, the sea, the dry land, God created vegetation, birds, fish, and animals. Then he created male and female in his image. This was life at its highest development. It was the crowning work of God's creation. After he created human male and female he looked at his creation and said it was *very good.* Thus God was expressing his divine approval, satisfaction, and enjoyment at the fulfillment of his creative purposes. Whereas the nonphysical part of man and woman (the soul, i.e., the mind, the emotions, the will) was created in the image and likeness of God, the physical part of man, his body, was created for functional needs of living in God's world. The Hebrew-Christian Scriptures describe the physical body and the nonphysical image of God as being a unit, in which the nonphysical self is in control of the physical body.

When God created male and female, man and woman, he created "sex" as a part of his total plan. The word *sex* is not in the Bible, yet on almost every page the Bible discusses what the word sex refers to when it describes relationships between men and women in family life. The word sex is an English translation of the Latin *sexus* which is derived from other Latin words meaning *to cut, to divide*. It refers to God's division of created life into two complementary units—male and female. Sex is the sum of the structural and functional differences by which male and female are distinguished.

Sex in the Bible

Even though the word *sex* is not in the Bible, the nature, the role, and the activities of human sexuality are freely and frankly discussed in sincere, honest, and dignified language. It was considered to be a part of God's creation and was therefore very personal and sacred. As a result, the Hebrew-Christian language selected words and phrases to describe sex that avoided concepts that might tend to lower the essential quality and effective power of divine moral standards intended by the Creator.

The Hebrew-Christian language refers to sexual intercourse indirectly in various descriptive terms. The Scriptures speak of the husband-wife sexual experience as *becoming one flesh* (Gen. 2:24, Mark 10:8, 1 Cor. 6:16). "*Lying* with a person" also refers to sexual intercourse (Gen. 34:7; Deut. 22:22). Other passages speak of sexual intercourse as a man *knowing* his wife (Gen. 4:1, 17, 25; Matt. 1:25). The writer of Hebrews refers to sexual intercourse when the *bed* is said to be honorable and undefiled in husband-wife relationships (Heb. 13:4). The apostle Paul describes the one-flesh relationship frankly with three different phrases: (1) *conjugal rights*, (2) *do not refuse one another*, and (3) *come together again* (1 Cor. 7:3, 5).

The Scriptures speak only indirectly of the male sex organs. Such words as *flesh, loin*, or *thigh* were used to refer to the male genitals (Gen. 17:11; 24:2, 9). Also the Scriptures use the word *loins* to refer to offspring coming from sexual organs (Gen. 35:11 KJV; Acts 2:30, KJV; and Heb. 7:10). In Deuteronomy 25:11, the male sex organs are called *private parts*.

The female sex organs are not referred to directly in the Scriptures. They are referred to indirectly in relationship to the total body (Lev. 18:7, 9; 20:17). The female *breasts* are spoken of in several passages such as Job 3:12, Song of Solomon 7:7–8, Ezekiel 16:7. The female *womb* is mentioned in many passages including Genesis 25:24; Proverbs 31:2; Isaiah 49:15; Luke 1:31; Romans 4:19. In the King James translation, the sexual desire of single women and widows is described as *burning*. The Revised Standard Version says *aflame with passion* (1 Cor. 7:9).

The word *seed* is used to refer to male semen in many places in the King James translation (Gen. 3:15; Lev. 22:4; Isa. 48:19). Some think that the female *ova* is implied in Genesis 3:15.[6]

In 1 Corinthians 7:2–5, Paul gives a detailed discussion of sexual intercourse in marriage. My free translation follows:

> Because of the strong nature of the sexual drive, each man should have his own wife, and each woman should have her own husband. The husband should regularly meet his wife's needs, and the wife should regularly meet her husband's needs. In marriage, just as the wife's body belongs to her husband and he rules over it, so in marriage, the husband's body belongs to his wife and she rules over it. Do not refuse to meet each other's sexual needs, unless you both agree to abstain from intercourse for a short time in order to devote yourselves to prayer. But because of your strong sexual drive, when this short period is passed, continue to meet each other's sexual needs by coming together again in sexual intercourse.

Thus the Old and New Testaments use selected words and phrases to refer to the sex organs and to sexual intercourse so as to veil and conceal the personal, sacred, and intimate nature of sexual union in marriage. Yet they indicate the Hebrew Christians had a clear knowledge and awareness of the nature of union through sexual intercourse involving pleasure and companionship between husband and wife. Some skeptics of Christian morals have asked, "Since the Hebrew Christians did not think sex was evil, why did they avoid using words that referred directly to male and female sex organs and sexual intercourse?" The reason is that the Creator did not intend the sexual experience in marriage to be simply a superficial, frivolous, random incident. Rather it was to be a profound, central, and foundational part of husband-wife relationships, around which other strands of their life experience were to be entwined. Sexual intercourse is so inherent, so essential, and so expressive in husband-wife interpersonal relationships, that it calls for loyalty, integrity, reverence, self-discipline, and moral reliability.

Because of its personal and sacred nature, human sexuality demands that we observe moral proprieties in dress and behavior in all social relationships and that husband and wife be withdrawn from the presence and/or observations of others when intimacies are consummated. These concepts of modesty and privacy do not mean that we think that sex is sinful, that we are embarrassed by it, or that we feel our conscience will blame us with guilt. Rather, they mean that one-flesh sexual experiences in marriage are very sacred, personal, and intimate. Sexual love requires personal seclusion; it loses divinely intended reality when observed by others.

The Purpose of Sex

First, God created male and female in his image and instructed them to have dominion over and subdue created life. Then he gave instructions about his purpose for the relationships in marriage. His intention is stated in precise and accurate language in Genesis 2:24: "Therefore a man leaves his father and his mother and cleaves to his wife, and they become one flesh." This passage is the heart, the touchstone, of God's intended purpose for a husband and his wife in their marriage relationship. The passage is confirmed and emphasized in the New Testament by both Jesus (Mark 10:2–12) and Paul (1 Cor. 6:16). This passage assigns a definite meaning and purpose to human sexuality. Husband and wife are to become *one flesh*.

What does this *one flesh* mean? The word *one* signifies *unity* between husband and wife. What kind of unity? It is a *one-flesh* unity. The word *flesh* has many different meanings in the Scriptures. Flesh, a translation of the Hebrew *basar* and Greek *sarx*, may mean (1) the soft part of the physical body, (2) the whole body, (3) the living being, (4) the human personality, (5) this earthly life, and (6) moral weakness and frailty of human nature, to name a few. Thus the meaning of the word *flesh* may be literal or figurative. The meaning must be determined by the context of the passage. What is the meaning of *one flesh* in Genesis 2:24? Here we have a relationship between two different persons, a wife and her husband. Jesus, in quoting the passage, said ". . . The two shall become one flesh. So they are no longer two but one" (Mark 10:8, NIV). In the science of numbers, one plus one equals two. Yet here Jesus says that one plus one equals one. He was not saying that the two separate personalities of a man and a woman become one personality. This would conflict with the biblical emphasis on the infinite worth of persons as seen in the teachings of Jesus. Certainly, it does not mean that two physical bodies become one physical body. Thus the meaning of one flesh in the passage must be figurative, not literal.

It is obvious from the context of the passage and the first chapters of Genesis that the term *one flesh* refers to sexual intercourse between husband and wife. It is also obvious from the context that one flesh has a wider meaning than just physical sexual intercourse. The concept of one flesh involves a union of the total man and the total woman. That is, it includes all of the physical and the nonphysical aspects of both. It brings the physical and the nonphysical together involving the whole personality of both individuals. Yes, it includes the pure physical pleasure of sexual intercourse. But this one-flesh reality is much, much more. The physical pleasure is surrounded by, caught up in, integrated, and blended with the spiritual, emotional, and mental aspects of personality in a deeper, more intense and profound response and experience of pleasure and delight. Following the one-flesh experience, both husband and wife are aware of the total fulfillment of the needs of their total personalities at a deeper level. It involves profound and sublime insight at the spiritual, emotional, moral, and intellectual levels.

In the one-flesh experience, husband and wife gain a new knowledge of each other and of themselves. Before the first sexual experience they can have a shadowy idea of the nature of sexual unity in marriage, but only in their sexual experience can they comprehend the full meaning of *one flesh*. The Bible uses the verb *ginasko* meaning "to know," "to know by experience" (Matt. 1:25). Thus in the one-flesh experience, the husband understands more fully the nature of his masculinity and his wife's femininity. The wife understands more fully the nature of her femininity and of her husband's masculinity. The inner nature of their sexuality is understood and reciprocated. The one-flesh completeness that God intended in creation is now achieved. Each has supplied something that completes the other and that completion reflects the image that God created in them. They are now wholly different from what they were before. The one-flesh experience symbolizes the mutual commitment that binds them together.

The one-flesh unity forms a new social unit, the family. Husband and wife leave their parents and cleave to each other.

3

Male and Female Created He Them

In addition to biblical revelation, let us make a study of the biological nature of human sexuality as planned by the Creator to help us come to grips with reality about our future as related to sex. In order to control our sexuality and allow it to function through future Christian marriage channels, we need to understand that the Creator created sex as a *strong drive in both men and women.* Although male and female have many differences in the expression of their sexual drive, the evidence indicates that God created them as sexual equals in need and pleasure.

A brief review of the sexual and reproductive systems of the male and the female should help us to further understand the nature of sex. We will call attention to the relationships of the sexual system and the reproductive system in both male and female.

In the human male, after puberty, the *testicles* are continually producing sperm cells. These cells are sent out into the *epididymis,* an external storage vessel adjacent to the testicles. When the epididymis is filled, during any type of sexual stimulation, the sperm are moved out of the epididymis through the *vas deferens* into the body cavity and deposited into the *seminal vesicles,* an internal storage vessel. Along the way, various fluids are added to the sperm. When the two storage vessels are filled, the man involved is sexually in need and anxious for a sexual release through an ejaculation of the semen. It is difficult to adequately describe the vigorous and increasing pressure of that need. A release can be triggered automatically through some type of stimulation of the penis such as wet dreams (a full bladder stimulates the seminal vesicles), self-release (masturbation), or sexual intercourse. Of course, when the semen is released through sexual intercourse into the vaginal passage, there is the possibility of pregnancy if female *ova* (egg cells) are present. This continuing process of male production of semen and its necessary release is inherent in all men. God created men thus (Gen. 1:27). It is God-given and natural! The process is not sinful! Of course, the misuse and abuse of this system is sinful. All of us need to understand the nature of this process and the regular inherent sexual need that God has created and deposited in men. In planning a marriage, a single woman needs to understand this nature of men to insure a successful sexual relationship in marriage. In past history, Christian thought has often ignored these facts concerning male sexuality, and that ignorance has been a major cause of much sexual immorality.

In like manner, we need to understand the sexual nature that God created and deposited in the human female (Gen. 1:27). He created her with two separate systems, the sexual system and the reproductive system. The two, although they cooperate with each other, are two separate systems with two separate functions. There is sufficient evidence for this in both male and female, but the evidence is most pronounced in the female. The evidence in the female is as follows.

(1) While the female reproductive system is an internal bodily system (ovaries, fallopian tubes, uterus, vagina), the female sexual system is an external system (clitoris, labia majora, labia minora). The *clitoris* is the sexual organ that triggers female sexual arousal and orgasm. It has no direct relationship to the process of reproduction.

(2) A woman does not have to experience a sexual orgasm to become pregnant.

(3) Research indicates that the average young wife after two years of marriage needs and would like to have sexual intercourse

on the average of every 3.2 days; a pregnancy, however, can occur only once every nine or ten months.

(4) When a woman has a hysterectomy, the removal of her uterus by surgical operation, her reproductive system ceases to function. But after recovery from such an operation, under normal conditions her sexual system continues to function the rest of her life.

(5) A woman's sexual need continues both during a pregnancy and during her menstrual cycle (reproductive process), sometimes at an increased rate.

(6) At menopause (age 45–50), the menstrual period and the process of reproduction cease, but a woman's sexual system continues to function normally the rest of her life and sometimes at an increased rate.

These facts concerning the relationship of a woman's sexual system and her reproductive system positively indicate that God created woman's sexual and reproductive systems as two separate systems with two separate functions. This is *positive evidence that the Creator-God planned for a woman to enjoy regular, normal, sexual experiences in marriage all her life*. This fact is in harmony with many passages of Scripture that discuss the sex life of husbands and wives (Gen. 2:24; Matt. 19:4–6; Mark 10:6–9; 1 Cor. 7:2–5; and Heb. 13:4).

Thus we must conclude that the Scriptures and scientific biological facts both teach that sex for the purpose of personal pleasure between husband and wife is within the plan of God for both man and woman.

4

In Defense of Marriage

We all want to know what the human male and female are meant to be. There are two opposing answers to this question. One approach assumes that a child is born with a "blank mind," that is, it has no knowledge or innate tendencies at birth. All of its future knowledge comes from without through experiences in social interaction. This view assumes that all sex differences are learned behavior. It recommends what sociologists call "role interchangeability" between male and female. It rightly emphasizes the importance of personhood. But the major problem with this view is that, although it gives lip service to God and biblical authority, it has long, deep roots that feed in the soil of humanism and take orders from that philosophy.

Most evangelicals prefer a different view in trying to understand what male and female were meant to be. We assume that, as a result of divine creation plans, a child is born with some innate tendencies. Therefore, we believe that, although some sex roles are learned, the basic sex roles rest upon divine creative purposes located in male and female sex differences. We believe (1) that in determining cultural roles we must retain and emphasize female uniqueness and male uniqueness, (2) that we must preserve biblical equality and a high and sacred ideal of male and female personhood, (3) that we need to develop a clear understanding of how female uniqueness and male uniqueness cooperate in a union of one flesh, and (4) that we need a clear definition of what male and female are meant to be. Let us search the Scriptures for light on these issues.

The Scriptures on Marriage

What does the Bible teach concerning male and female relationships? The Old Testament reveals that in creation, God's original purpose for the male-female relationship was marriage (Gen. 2:24). The Hebrew mind regarded marriage as sacred and under God's order and control. By definition, the word *marriage,* as used in this book, means one man and one woman living together as husband and wife during their lifetime.

Immediately after creation, God called for marriage (Gen. 2:24). In Hebrew thought, happiness was related to marriage (Ps. 128; Prov. 31). Marriage is used as a metaphor to describe the ideal union between God and Israel. The fifth commandment, "Honor your father and mother," assumes marriage as its foundation. It is saying that parenthood is honorable and that parents must be honorable. The seventh commandment, "You shall not commit adultery," assumes and defends marriage. The tenth commandment, "You shall not covet your neighbor's wife," assumes marriage. Moses, the prophets, Jesus, and the apostles defended and promoted marriage.

The Meaning of One 'Flesh'

Central in the biblical doctrine of marriage is the *one-flesh* doctrine. What is the essential character and nature of the one-flesh relationship that God planned and created for male and female? It is a relationship which completes and fulfills them and brings glory to him.

In fornication, the conditions necessary for establishing the one-flesh experience are not present. There is no *agape* love. There are no plans for fidelity. There are no plans for sharing life together. There is no recognition of responsibility for each other or the community. Derrick Sherwin Bailey says the aspects of fornication "merely enact a hollow, ephemeral, diabolical parody of marriage which works disintegration of the personality and leaves behind a deeply seated sense of frustration and dissatisfaction."[7]

On the negative side, the consent to marry, the legal document, and the marriage ceremony, do not constitute one-flesh reality. Although these do not constitute one-flesh unity, they are important and necessary prerequisites to marriage.

The following is a paraphrase of Bailey's description of the things necessary for marriage.

1. A man and woman love each other with *agape* love.
2. They both consent to marriage.
3. They mutually proceed freely, deliberately, and responsibly in planning their marriage.
4. The community is informed of the marriage and approves it.
5. They conform to divine law (whether they know it or not).
6. They give themselves to each other in sexual intercourse.[8]

It is the experience of sexual intercourse that establishes the one-flesh unity. The experience involves two persons who are complete in themselves being combined into another complete functioning unit. They become a part of each other and participate in each other's nature, yet they retain their own individuality and identity.

It is not enough to say that in the one-flesh experience husband and wife are now uniting and cooperating for common goals and purposes. It is that, but it is more. It is a personal, sacred experience in which two dimensions—the physical reality and the spiritual-mental-emotional reality—are combined into one reality. It is not a reality in the sense of becoming another person. It is a reality, a truth, in the sense that it can be known in experience but cannot be fully understood by human reason. It is more than a symbolic something. It will help us to understand the mystery of one flesh to see that it is similar to the reality of the unity of a person participating in Christ's nature through repentance and faith, or to the reality of the unity of Christ and the church.

Jesus' Teachings on Marriage

Jesus' teachings concerning marriage followed the teaching of Moses and the prophets. He sanctioned the Genesis account of creation as authority for marriage (Matt. 19:3–6). Everywhere in his teaching he accepted marriage and treated it as sacred and divine. He attended a wedding in Cana of Galilee and participated in the activities of the evening by performing his first recorded miracle (John 2:1–11). Thus he sanctioned marriage. He used the institution of marriage in figures of speech to illustrate his central teachings concerning the kingdom of God (Matt. 25:1–13). He did allow divorce in case of adultery (Matt. 19:3–9). This exception was in line with his teaching of grace, mercy, and justice. But he had a stern, uncompromising view of adultery, a view that stressed the importance of the marriage relationship (Matt. 5:27–28).

Paul's Teachings on Marriage

Paul's concept of marriage has been greatly distorted by enemies of the Bible and by shallow Bible interpretation. In his advice to the Corinthian church, Paul was not saying that marriage is only for those who cannot control their sex drive. He was not saying that the married are weak and that those who stay single are strong. Rather he was saying that one of the values of marriage is that it allows divinely approved expression of the sexual desire that is a part of the gift of creation. Both Jesus (Matt. 19:11) and Paul (1 Cor. 7:6–9) were saying that to be able to live a wholesome life without the necessity for sexual expression was a special gift and not the norm for male and female. Positively, Paul emphasized marriage as being honorable and within the will of God (1 Cor. 7:2–5; 1 Thess. 4:1–8). He compared the union of husband and wife to the relationship of Christ and the church by saying that husbands and wives should be subject to and love one another as the church is subject to and loves Christ (Eph. 5:21–25). He sanctioned marriage when he pleaded with parents to bring their children up in the nurture and admonition of the Lord (Eph. 6:4).

Paul sternly condemned fornication, adultery, and homosexuality—the sexual sins that undermine and destroy marriage. He warned young Timothy to beware of false teachers who would "depart from the faith by giving heed to deceitful spirits and doctrines of demons . . . who forbid marriage . . . which God created to be received with thanksgiving by those who believe and know the truth. For everything created by God is good, and nothing is to be rejected" (1 Tim. 4:1–4).

Thus the Bible calls for marriage as the only system of male-female relationship that produces a stable family life and gives a proper organizational foundation for civilization and the growth of the kingdom of God.

Biological Evidences for Marriage

In addition to the Scriptures calling for marriage, there are four biological evidences flowing from God's creation that call for marriage.

1. In most animals, sex is practiced in season for reproduction, but in human beings sex is a continuous force and is practiced both for pleasure and reproduction. This fact assumes marriage.
2. During pregnancy and the nursing period, others must supply the mother and the child with their needs—food, clothing, and shelter. Thus a permanent marriage arrangement is needed for survival.
3. The prolonged period of human infancy requires a permanent economic and social arrangement. Marriage meets this need.
4. At birth the sexes are approximately balanced, with an equal number of boy babies and girl babies. The Creator seems to be asking for marriage. When the number of the sexes gets off balance, it is not the fault of the Creator, but rather the fault of corrupt and depraved social and political practices of given cultures.

Social Advantages of Marriage

1. Marriage meets the life needs of women. It provides the relationship necessary to meet their emotional, social, sexual, economic, moral, and spiritual needs. It gives women the highest status possible. Every married woman is the queen of her family, and her home is her castle.

2. Marriage meets the needs of men. The idea that one wife cannot meet the total sexual needs of one husband is a primitive myth grounded in ignorance. Marriage gives man the highest possible status. In marriage, every man is the king of his family, and his home is his castle.

3. Marriage meets the needs of children. The normal personality growth and development of children calls for love, empathy, understanding, and the care of both their father and their mother. Institutional or communal care is not enough. History is replete with examples of impersonal care or outright neglect which gradually eroded and stunted the lives of children. Nor can children receive the affection and leadership they need when one or both parents are promiscuously involved in sex relations with persons other than their spouse.

4. People have a social right and need to know who their relatives are. A wife has a right to know who the father of her children is. A husband has a right to know that he is the father of his children. Children have a right to know who their father is. Marriage makes these rights possible.

5. Marriage affords the privacy necessary for the operation of love, empathy, and understanding in husband/wife relationships and interfamily relationships.

Spiritual, Mental, and Emotional Advantages of Marriage

1. Joanna Magda Polenz in her excellent book *In Defense of Marriage* believes that the permanence and exclusiveness of marriage form a strong bond and give strength and magic to marriage.

She feels that marriage is liberating while singleness is constricting. She says, "Relieved from sexual pressure and with the security of having a loved person with whom to pool resources, married people find that they can devote more time and energy to work than they could as single people."[9]

2. In the later years, married people have the fellowship and the loving arms, words, and deeds of their children and grandchildren that provide emotional security.

3. As husband and wife grow older in marriage, they can stay sexually active longer.

4. Marriage brings a pleasant attitude and feeling of security and happiness as husband and wife change and mature across the years.

5. Marriage presents the best possible social situation to avoid loneliness. In our study of 608 singles, the word *loneliness* was most frequently mentioned as a problem. One said, "It is a very lonely life, with little to look forward to. In my loneliness, I bathe myself in my own tears."

6. Marriage is uniquely prepared to give ready, effective, and supportive service to every member of the family in time of emergency or disaster. Polenz says, "At the heart of the capacity to support a spouse is the positive relationship that exists on so many levels when people are happily wed. Even in fortunate times, people function better when they have love, security, companionship, and a sexual outlet."[10]

Some Reasons People Do Not Marry

In light of the fact that God through revelation and nature presents marriage as the norm for male and female, what are some of the reasons that people do not marry? Some people, both male and female, feel duty bound to care for their invalid parents. They would love to be married and have a secret longing for it, but choose to remain single and lovingly care for parents as long as they live. This is in line with the principle of the fifth commandment (Exod. 20:12). When parents are gone, often many years have passed, the single person is now middle-aged or past, and some undesirable personality patterns may have developed. Some of the best possible years for marriage are gone and there are few if any remaining prospects, especially for women.

Some Christian youth grow up in small rural communities where there are few prospects. Many of the possible prospects are unacceptable for understandable reasons. Family loyalty and work responsibilities may cause such people to remain at home in a social situation where the chances for a good marriage elude them.

In the past, our patriarchal society has said that only the man should take the initiative in courtship. This concept has taught women to be passive and wait to be asked. Some women are never asked. One said on her questionnaire, "I have never had a date."

Some young men and women grow up shy and reserved around the opposite sex. In their inexperience, they are somewhat afraid of courtship, marriage, and sex. Secretly they want to be married but hesitate to follow through on potential opportunities.

Others develop perfectionistic personalities and, as they think about marriage, they set up such extremely high standards for the characteristics of what a marriage prospect should have that a marriage is not possible. There is the story of someone who said to a bachelor friend, "Why haven't you married?" He replied, "I am looking for a perfect wife." "And did you find one?" "Yes," he replied. "Then why did you not marry her?" He responded, "She was looking for a perfect husband."

Some religious singles get locked into singleness through extreme Calvinistic fatalism—the belief that all human events are fixed in advance so that persons are powerless to change them. On the questionnaire one respondent said, "If God wants me to meet someone and marry, I will. If not, I'll live each day as it comes." Another said, "If marriage happens, it happens. If it doesn't, it doesn't. And that is still O.K." These singles really want to marry but their religious belief paralyzes their initiative, and they accept a passive role. They sit down in singleness and wait for God to set someone in their lap and pull the marriage trigger. Of course, ardent faith in God is indeed essential, but such passive fatalism contradicts such Bible passages as Genesis 2:24, Philippians 2:12–13. (Chapter 14 will discuss the subject of taking the initiative in finding a marriage partner.)

Many handicapped people are shut out of possible marriage because of society's concept that they should never marry. Let us assume that there are certain extremely handicapped people who should not marry for their own good and the good of society. Yet, the fact remains that thousands of persons with handicaps have a right to marry. Handicapped persons are *persons.* We are all thankful that the writings of some evangelicals are now defending marriage for the handicapped. Most handicapped men and women want marriage, have a right to marry, and are worthy of it.

Many people are concerned about the high divorce rate in our society. In growing up, some have experienced the trauma of the divorce of their parents or brothers and sisters, and have become afraid of possible marriage. Their fears have been fanned by the secular media, movies, and television that often gleefully accept and encourage divorce. Such fears cause them to doubt the institution of marriage.

The social life of many people is blocked by the lack of self-confidence and self-esteem. They are insecure persons who want marriage but lack the courage to take the initiative, or they repel marriage prospects because of strange attitudes and personalities. (The importance of self-esteem is discussed in Chapter 11.)

Some people develop social relationships with a small group of close friends of the same sex and tend to hibernate with them. These friendships tend to crystallize into a clique. Held together by a presumed identity of interests and views, such a group forms a narrow, exclusive circle around itself and tends to reject or ignore others. The smug attitude of these groups tends to repel marriage prospects.

Conclusions

In the past, we Christians have been so conditioned by the erotic sexuality of our culture that we have interpreted the male and female one-flesh relationship as being largely physical and have overlooked its spiritual-mental-emotional dimension. With a biblical understanding of the marriage relationship, a husband and wife can have happiness and a life of service together that they never could have had as two separate persons. The knowledge that each succeeding act of sexual intercourse maintains a state of one flesh between them keeps their committed love, trust, and respect continually flowing back and forth. When children come into the home, these continued one-flesh relationships, attitudes, feelings, and motives keep love, trust, and respect flowing from parents to children and from children back to parents. The evidence indicates that marriage develops personality, human happiness, and meets social needs to the maximum. The benefits flowing from it are the spiritual, moral, social, and economic building blocks of civilization, human life, and the kingdom of God. Marriage is demanded by the realities of human existence and human need. Marriage pictures what male and female relationships were intended to be.

5

In Defense of Singles

To understand singles as they are in our culture and to help them understand themselves, I conducted two fact-finding projects. First I made a study of 608 never-married people, age twenty-five and up who lived in twenty-five states, predominantly Tennessee and surrounding states. I sent out a fifty-four item questionnaire and received the replies by mail. Second, I conducted fourteen two-hour seminars with never-married singles, ages twenty-five to forty, with an average attendance of ten. One week before each session, members of the seminar were given copies of a chapter of this manuscript to be discussed. They were encouraged to study it critically. During each seminar session, we read the chapter aloud and then discussed the positive and negative merits of it.

In my study of 608 never-married people, 78 percent of both men and women said they would, under ideal circumstances, consider marriage for themselves now. Several who would not consider marriage for themselves now were either those who were ages twenty-five to thirty and planned marriage later or those who were from age sixty-five up who indicated they had considered marriage when they were younger. Thus our research confirms the Gallup Poll findings that 90 percent of American men and women prefer marriage.

Since most men and women prefer marriage, why are there so many people in our society who have never married? In our study, when singles were asked which of the following three was the basic cause of their being single, 89 percent said "myself," 5 percent said "my parents," and 6 percent said "society at large."

When they were asked to check the three items out of sixteen, in the order of importance (1, 2, and 3) that most nearly gave the reason for their not being married, the following received the ten highest ratings:

1. I never did meet the person I wanted to marry.
2. I preferred personal independence to marriage.
3. My expectations were too high.
4. I did not marry because of an inner reason that I do not know how to explain.
5. I was deeply hurt by someone I loved and lost faith in the opposite sex.
6. I have simply been too timid.
7. I waited for greater financial security.
8. My education deferred my marriage until eligible prospects had married.
9. The demands of my occupation made marriage inadvisable.
10. I was afraid of the fact that so many marriages end in divorce.

Some Reasons for Singleness Examined

Six percent of people in our sample blamed *society* for their being single. These replies at best are only a part-truth. In the strictest sense, society does not make our decisions for us. Society can influence us, but it does not mechanically determine our decisions. Only individual persons make decisions. I feel that much of the unhappiness of singles (or married people) is the result of free choices and bad decisions on the part of the individuals involved.

In the research, a few people said that the high *divorce rate* caused them to question the wisdom of marriage. This assumes that marriage as a social institution is defective. This is questionable thinking. The real problem is not marriage as a way of life. Human pride, greed, lust, and other self-centered traits of husbands and wives are the real cause for divorce. But the institution of marriage is not the culprit. Marriage is inherent in the created nature of male and female.

Some people say that marriage is "*so final.*" Yes, this is true, but isn't singleness equally final? This objection to marriage seems to indicate that the person involved is not quite sure which is preferable, singleness or marriage. If a mature Christian has sought God's will and leadership in the choices of life and of one's life companion, he need not fear the finality of the relationship.

The pseudo-religious belief that says, "If you have *Jesus,* you don't need a husband or wife; Jesus can meet all your needs," needs to be carefully examined. Yes, this statement is partly true, but it neglects much significant truth. In singleness, one has to forego the fulfillment of certain needs. God created man and woman in his image with spiritual, emotional, and physical needs. These needs and the processes through which they are to be met were divinely created and are good. These needs cannot be adequately met except in marriage with another human being of the opposite sex. I fear those who say, "If you have Jesus, you don't need a marriage companion," are pushing sex aside and refusing to deal with it. This is dangerous. When sexual desire is repressed, it may fester and later express itself in various emotional and personality quirks or even moral problems.

Sincere Servant Singles

My research and seminars seem to indicate that the never-married largely fall into three general categories. The first category I will call the *sincere servant singles.* They are singles who feel a definite call to give themselves in a life of sacrificial service to promoting the gospel of Christ and the kingdom of God. They want to be what Paul called servants—bond-slaves of Jesus Christ. They are very sincere, honest, warm, enthusiastic Christians. Single missionaries, some church staff members, and some lay people could be considered in this category.

The Scriptures on Singleness

What does the Bible have to say about sincere servant singles? Marriage was the common life style in the Scriptures. However, scattered throughout the Old and the New Testaments were some people who either by choice or life circumstances spent some time in a state of singleness. In the Old Testament there were Hagar, Deborah, Isaac, Dinah, Miriam, Naomi, and Jeremiah; in the New Testament, Anna, John the Baptist, Paul, and Jesus. When we search the Old Testament, it is difficult to find evidence in defense of singleness. In fact, the Old Testament does not have a word for "bachelor." The New Testament, however, is a different story. Jesus and Paul both have definite teachings in defense of singleness.

Jesus on Singleness

In Jesus' discussion with the Pharisees about divorce, he went behind Old Testament divorce rules (Deut. 24:1–4) and built his reply on God's plan in creating man and woman (Gen. 1:27, 2:24). He called for permanent marriage (Matt. 19:3–9). Later, privately, in the home of John Mark, his disciples asked him, "Is it better not to marry?" They were implying that if the ties of marriage are so strict that there can be no way to get out of it except through adultery or death, maybe it would be better to stay single. They were assuming that a woman could have many other faults as bad as adultery. The disciples seemed reluctant to give up the Jewish pattern of easily getting rid of a wife. Jesus, recognizing their question as being in line with the selfish, worldly view of marriage of the males in their day, said:

> Not all men can receive this saying, but only those to whom it is given. There are eunuchs who have been so from birth, and there are

eunuchs who have been made eunuchs by men, and there are eunuchs who have made themselves eunuchs for the sake of the kingdom of heaven. He who is able to receive this, let him receive it (Matt. 19:11–12).

Jesus was saying that believers who feel divinely called ("to whom it is given") to do so, may take up singleness voluntarily as a vocation for *one spiritual purpose only, that is, the advancement of the kingdom of God.* He was saying they must volunteer to practice self-mastery and self-control, including complete abstinence from marriage and sexual intercourse. In this passage, Jesus did not approve of choosing singleness for ascetic reasons (sex is evil), as some have assumed. He said singleness is only for the person "who is able," that is, has the capacity of meeting the high moral demands of singleness, including subduing and suppressing sexual desire and need. Jesus' language seems to imply that this is *very difficult* for any person to do. Note that he did not say that either marriage or singleness is morally superior or inferior. But Jesus did defend sincere servant singles.

Paul on Singleness

Paul said in reply to the marriage problems of the Corinthian Christians (1 Cor. 7), (1) "It is good for a man not to marry" (verse 1, NIV), (2) "Now to the unmarried and the widows I say it is good for them to stay unmarried, as I am" (verse 8, NIV), and (3) in talking to unmarried people, he says, "But if you, a man, should marry, don't think you have done anything sinful. And the same applies to a young woman. Yet I do believe that those who take this step are bound to find the married state an extra burden *in these critical days*" (verse 28, Phillips, italics added).

We may summarize Paul's attitude toward singleness in the context of chapter 7 as follows:

1. His ideas about singleness are his opinion and not from divine command (verse 25).

2. He is living the single life and wishes others could do so, but does not attempt to force singleness on anyone.

3. He thinks both marriage and singleness are good. Neither is superior or inferior. Neither is sinful in itself.

4. His advice about singleness was influenced by his thoughts that the second coming of Christ was at hand and would be accompanied by very critical times (1 Cor. 7:26). This was major in determining his thinking about singleness.

5. Paul did defend sincere servant singles.

In view of the Persian and Greek false doctrine of asceticism (the spirit is good, the flesh is evil), plus the asceticism of some of the early church fathers (including Ambrose and Augustine), it is easy to read into Paul's ideas about singleness a greater emphasis than is justified. Marriage was never officially condemned by the Old or New Testament leaders. After the close of the New Testament, Persian and Greek philosophy influenced the early church, and the idea that virginity was the purest state for male and female took root and was sanctioned and encouraged by some of the church fathers. Three levels of spiritual purity were gradually developed: (1) absolute virginity was the highest and the purest level of spirituality; (2) a lower spiritual level was celibacy (singleness), practiced by those who had been formerly married; (3) the lowest spiritual level was marriage. But this whole ascetic system is rejected by both the Old and New Testaments. We must guard against reading this false system of thought back into the teachings of Jesus and Paul as many have done in the history of Christendom.

Now, in view of the teaching of Jesus and Paul concerning singleness and marriage, what conclusions can be reached? Those who are looking for proof texts can present a good case for either marriage or singleness from the Scriptures. Both Jesus and Paul commended singleness under certain circumstances as being good and not evil. Paul tells us that a single person can have more time and energy to serve the kingdom of God (1 Cor. 7:32–35). Also, he was sympathetic to the single and to the widowed and extended to them mercy, grace, and empathy (1 Cor. 7:8).

The Scriptures teach that for some special service, God may call certain individuals (sincere servant singles) to a life of singleness when such a status best suits the fulfillment of that particular service. Those who respond to this calling should understand (1) that certain personal fulfillments are thus rendered impossible, (2) that the Lord Jesus is able to compensate for these deficiencies in other ways, (3) that such a life may be flooded with many and varied temptations, (4) that the single life of service should not necessarily cause a warped and twisted personality, and (5) that such a life status is for one purpose only: to render special service to the kingdom of God.

Self-Centered Secular Singles

At the other extreme, our research and seminars revealed a small, articulate and influential group of singles that I will call *self-centered secular singles.* They are largely educated people, both men and women, who enjoy freedom and independence. They are saying, "I want self-fulfillment. I want to be me. I want to do my own thing." And, "I want to live my own life." I am going to allow them to describe themselves in their own language from the replies on the questionnaires:

Getting married is such a sacrifice now.

It costs so much money and time to raise children.

I am happy alone, also somewhat selfish.

I like lots of different women in my bed.

I can live with my life style as is and be fulfilled without marriage and a family.

To some extent, I just don't like women. I am not that interested in the mating game. I don't like the way that God set this area of life up.

Singleness means learning values, how to support yourself; being free to make choices and exercise one's own judgment without conflict with a spouse.

You are independent to travel, make your own decisions, right or wrong, and grow as a person.

I enjoy being single. I am responsible only to myself; I enjoy doing things myself. Friends are all right at times, but not marriage.

I cherish solitude and I cherish intimacy. When I have a relationship with a man that satisfies me with needed love, then I may plan to live with him—and marry.

I enjoy being single . . . am perfectly happy—enjoy going where I please, when I please, doing whatever I please—I have passed up several opportunities for marriage.

I am too independent to marry. I prefer to be able to go and do as I please and not have to answer to anyone.

Social Situation Singles

From my research and seminar data, there is a large segment of the never-married whom I will call *social situation singles*. They are those who would like to be married, but find themselves locked into a social situation that up to now has left them with little opportunity for marriage or kept them from marriage. Many of them are committed, practicing Christians who want to follow Christian moral guidelines. These social situations and the values and attitudes flowing from them vary greatly. Some of them are: caring for sick or invalid parents, growing up in a small community, attaching self to a small clique of the same sex, believing an extreme doctrine of fatalism, lacking self-confidence and self-esteem, being shy and bashful, being a perfectionist, having a physical or emotional handicap, being afraid of sex, reproduction and parenthood, being afraid of the high divorce rate.

Practical Considerations for Singles

A person who has not yet found a marriage partner should look at the positive aspects of the single life, while continuing plans toward a possible future marriage. If one has a positive and healthy attitude toward life, doors may open to marriage. It has happened to thousands.

These people have freedom to use their time as they wish, spend their money as they wish, and live and eat where they wish. However, they must guard against their independence breeding self-centeredness and inflexibility. The give-and-take situation of having a housemate can help ward against this tendency.

These people can give full attention to developing a career. They can give undivided attention to the community task they feel God has called them to do. Here again is a possible danger. One can easily become a workaholic and neglect other personal needs.

Such people have opportunities to develop a wide variety of talents and skills. They have to be able to do everything around the home: manage finances, keep a car and household appliances in working order, balance a checkbook, sew, cook, wash, and so on. All of this develops some self-confidence because they have to make decisions on their own and learn by experience.

Single people can develop deeper friendships on a broader scale. Such a person's life can be enriched because the scope of friends is usually more varied—young and old, married and single. They can develop deeper friendships for which the average married person often lacks time, physical and emotional energy. When married, it is easy to be satisfied with the friendships and companionship of one's spouse and children and make little effort to build friendships outside the home.

It is true that there are positive aspects of the single life, and these should be utilized. On the other hand, one should avoid overselling singleness. Many of us have the feeling that singleness is oversold in a variety of books, magazines, and newspapers on singleness. One person said, "I am a little bothered with the church and literature trying so hard to make us feel normal that they make us feel abnormal. Cliff Allbritton warns against a

> smug, nonchalant attitude toward the holy estate of matrimony. It is one thing to be single. It is quite another to be arrogant about it. . . . I have observed never marrieds and singles exaggerating to their mar-

ried friends about "the great time" they are having, "rubbing it in" and "overselling" their "fantastic" single lifestyle, intentionally creating doubt and dissatisfaction in the minds of the married listeners. Let us not forget that "each of us shall give account of himself to God" (Rom. 14:12) for our words and our influence.

As Christians, we are committed to the truth: that it is O.K. to be single, that we can be whole and experience the abundant life while single, that we should accept our singleness. At the same time, let's be honest about all our feelings. There are times when most of us would gladly trade in our singleness for the right mate and join the ranks of the married.

Let us learn the difference between the giddy, thin, half-true smoke-screen about singleness which flows from the insecurity and hollowness of the empty self and the solid acceptance and contentment with one's singleness which is grounded and anchored in the person of Jesus Christ. Let's tell the whole truth about our singleness and not try to oversell it.[11]

I have a "gut" feeling that *some of today's singles who hesitatingly classify themselves as sincere servant singles are really social situation singles who have honestly determined to follow Christ while they wait for possible marriage.* Down deep they feel that marriage answers the question of what male and female were meant to be.

Summary of Research

The following basic thought trends are reflected in our study of 608 never-married people.

1. Although not averse to marrying eventually, some with a higher education, a satisfying career, desire to travel, and so on, put marriage on the back burner.

2. Many are very sensitive and on the defensive about being single, yet would like to be married.

3. A few definitely prefer the single life style to marriage.

4. Some would like to be married, but, afraid of becoming

trapped in an unhappy marriage, are learning to accept singleness as a viable alternative.

5. The largest number deeply desire marriage and long for it to come to pass.

6. There was considerable evidence that men are as anxious about marriage as women. This may be understood in light of the strong, male sex drive and the fact that society has taught men to take the initiative in courtship.

7. Those who express opposition to marriage tend to overlook or ignore the biblical, biological, and spiritual-mental-emotional aspects of what male and female were intended to be.

PART II

Coping with Sexual Needs until Marriage

6

Sex Before Marriage

In view of the biblical and biological purpose and nature of the human sexual drive and need, singles face a major question: "How can we cope with our sexual needs and overcome problems related to sexual drive during singleness within the context of Christian sexuality?" We now come face to face with the question at the heart of this book, whether planning a permanent single life or marriage: how can never-married singles, the widowed, and the divorced utilize their sexuality for their spiritual, emotional, and physical well-being?

In our society, the secular culture encourages sexual promiscuity while Christian teachings call for sexual control until marriage. Courting couples are continually bombarded by the media in favor of promiscuity; as a result, they often find it difficult to understand the Christian concept of self-control. Thus, many are confused and torn between these two options. What do the Scriptures teach about sex before marriage?

The Old Testament

There are many Old Testament passages relating to the Hebrews' attitudes toward sex before marriage. The message comes through strongly and clearly that sexual intercourse is for marriage only, with strict penalties for those who violate this principle (Deut. 22:13–29). A girl who was not a virgin at the time of marriage was discriminated against (Deut. 22:28–29 and Exod. 22:16–17). The Old Testament sternly condemns the sin of harlotry (prostitution) (Lev. 19:20–21, 21:9, Prov. 6:24–26, 23:27–28, 29:3). These scriptures vividly state the concept that sex belongs to marriage.

There are two Old Testament descriptions of rape involving Shechem and Dinah (Gen. 34:1–31) and Amnon and Tamar (2 Sam. 13:11–22). The language describing these experiences definitely indicates rejection of sexual intercourse before marriage as well as a rejection of rape and incest.

In describing the sins of Israel against God, the prophet Amos says, "Fallen, no more to rise, is the virgin Israel" (Amos 5:2). Amos, in looking for language to describe wickedness of the continuous sins of Israel against God, selects the metaphor of a "fallen virgin." Once again, Scripture clearly indicates that the Hebrew prophet looked upon the virginity of an unmarried woman as the epitome of righteousness, and conversely, he looked upon sex relations before marriage as the epitome of evil.

The New Testament

There are two basic words used in the New Testament to describe sexual evil. The familiar word *adultery* (*moichaomai*), used many times, refers to all illicit sexual intercourse between married people. The second word *fornication* (*porneia*) is used over thirty times in the New Testament. Its basic meaning is sexual intercourse between unmarried people.

In 1 Corinthians 7:2 and in 1 Thessalonians 4:3–4 (this meaning is clearer in the Revised Standard Version) the word *fornication* refers to voluntary sexual intercourse between two unmarried people, or between an unmarried person and a married person. In both passages Paul uses the word fornication to *warn* unmarried people against the temptation of sexual intercourse before marriage. In both cases, he advocates marriage to replace a single life of sexual promiscuity.

In three passages, the words *adultery* and *fornication* are both used in describing sexual evil (Matt. 15:19; Mark 7:21; 1 Cor. 6:9, KJV). The contexts of these passages indicate a definite distinction between the two words. Since adultery refers to illicit sexual intercourse between married people, it follows that the word *fornication,* as used in these three passages, has to refer to sexual intercourse between single people. Thus these three passages warn against sexual intercourse outside of marriage as being evil. In the seven lists of evils which appear in the writings of the apostle Paul, the word *fornication* is included in five of them (1 Cor. 5:11, 1 Cor. 6:9; Gal. 5:19; Eph. 5:3; Col. 3:5), and it heads the list each time it is mentioned.

In some New Testament passages the word *fornication* has a wider meaning. The Greek *porneia* in these passages is usually translated by the words *immorality* and *unchastity* (1 Cor. 5:1). The word *porneia,* in these instances, may refer to all illicit sexual intercourse or to all sexual immorality in general. However, we point out that in twenty-three passages, this wider, general meaning *always includes* the concept of sexual intercourse of an unmarried person with anyone. Thus, the New Testament contains five direct references and twenty-three indirect references to the evils of sexual intercourse before marriage.

Fornication is listed in the same sentences with other sins such as idolatry, adultery, homosexuality, stealing, drunkenness, greed, selfishness, and envy. Following these listings, we are warned not to be deceived, for "the unrighteous shall not inherit the kingdom of God" (1 Cor. 6:9, KJV; Gal. 5:19).

Some critics have said that Jesus never had anything to say about sexual control before marriage. If that is true, what was he talking about when he said in the Sermon on the Mount, "But I say unto you that every one who looks at a woman lustfully has already committed adultery with her in his heart" (Matt. 5:28)? The words *every one* include singles and marrieds. Note that in this passage Jesus equates fornication with adultery.

When we look objectively at the Old and New Testaments, we see that the Judeo-Christian concept was that marriage was the only proper sexual relationship for men and women. The Scriptures firmly and unequivocally describe sexual intercourse before marriage as evil—a violation of the will of God.

What About Bodily Contact During Courtship?

In light of this biblical teaching, how then should the never-married deal with the problem of bodily contact during the processes of courtship? The ultimate purpose of courtship is for the selection of a future wife or husband. It involves social interaction that seeks to win the favor and affection of the sweetheart. Courtship includes some play and fun in the mutual effort of each to attract and win the favor of the other. It involves the matching and testing of values, beliefs, philosophies, and personalities. Each one studies the other's traits, habits, and character, and observes the other's attitudes toward devotion to Christ and commitment to the will of God.

The very nature of courtship involves some bodily contact. Bodily contact includes some sexual stimulation. Certainly at the proper time, place, circumstances, age, and with the proper understanding and restraint, some love expression involving bodily contact in courtship is normal. It is within Christian moral guidelines. During serious courtship, handholding and kissing, with no sexual strings attached, may be enjoyed by both. On the other hand, the never-married person who insists upon unrestrained, free bodily contact may be sure that fornication and its attendant adversities wait in ambush nearby. Therein lies the problem.

Bodily contact during courtship that includes sexual arousal, has often been called "making out" or "petting." Burgess and Locke refer to petting as physical contact between a man and a woman for the purpose of sexual arousal, stopping short of sexual intercourse. Landis and Landis are very realistic when they define petting as nature's plan for husband and wife in making preparation for sexual intercourse. Some writers classify petting on three levels: (1) necking (kissing and embracing), (2) light petting (caressing the physical body inside the clothing), and (3) heavy petting (stimulation of the genitals). For the purpose of this discussion, let us assume these definitions of light and heavy petting.

A Hit-and-Run Policy

In courtship, the desire to touch and caress the beloved is normal. Some have suggested a hit-and-run policy as being helpful. To illustrate, let us imagine that a mature couple, seriously going steady, has had a well-planned date and an enjoyable evening of social relationship. As they return home, they want and plan for some privacy before saying good night. During the privacy, they may feel free to give themselves to each other in embracing and kissing for a few fleeting moments. But soon they must say good night, and as they go their way, each is overflowing with emotional joy and happiness. They both have said by their embrace, "I love you" and "I accept and receive your love." There are no guilt feelings. Instead, there is a mountain-top feeling of joy and happiness. This type of hit-and-run policy is within Christian moral norms. It is not petting! It allows freedom with self-control. It does not provoke temptation.

On the other hand, excessive physical contact in the form of light or heavy petting is a violation of many Bible passages on sexual self-control. Petting arouses sexual impulses and leaves couples unsatisfied. When a couple begin to experiment with petting, they usually become more deeply involved with each successive experience. As with drug abuse, the amount and intensity of petting must be increased each time until total exhilaration is impossible short of intercourse. Even sexual intercourse before marriage cannot fully satisfy because it lacks the mental, emotional, and spiritual elements inherent in a marriage relationship between two people *committed* to one another.

Thus we see, petting is but a short, easy step to sexual intercourse and the major problems involved. Excessive bodily contact outside of marriage is sex as an end-in-itself. It is an overemphasis on the physical, the use of another person as a means to selfish ends, and the violation of the other person even if he or she freely consents. Persons are sacred and holy in God's plan and are not to be violated.

Petting to Orgasm

Some couples, insistent upon their freedom, continue petting but agree that they will keep their moral convictions and will always stop short of sexual intercourse. At each successive encounter they go a little further, and there is subsequently no place to stop, short of sexual release. Eventually, in their freedom of self-expression, they practice petting to orgasm and rationalize that they have not had sexual intercourse, that they are not guilty of sexual sin, and that they are both still virgins. This rationalization is self-deception. (We gullible human beings are past masters at self-deception, used to satisfy our own pride, greed and lust.) Such a couple is attributing their behavior to wise and credible motives without analyzing their true motives. They are providing seemingly plausible, but false reasons for their conduct, saying that if the girl's hymen is not broken, they are virgins, and that the sin of fornication involves only the breaking of the hymen in sexual intercourse To follow this line of reasoning makes the couple "legalists" in the sense of the scribes and Pharisees of the New Testament.

But the fact is they have done everything normal to sexual intercourse except breaking the hymen. Fornication, however, is something far more involved. In discussing couples petting to climax before marriage, Tim Stafford says,

> I think it relates to a kind of complete sexual intimacy: total "nakedness" toward each other, physically and emotionally. . . . I think petting to climax builds the same kind of intimacy and sharing between you. You are totally "naked" before each other; there is nothing held back.[12]

Petting to climax is God's plan for married couples to use in sexual love expression when conditions over which they have no control make it unwise to have sexual intercourse. This is right and good. This same process before marriage is fornication.

Bible Passages on Sexual Control

We have said that physical contact during courtship in the form of light or heavy petting is a violation of Bible passages on sexual control. Here we need to recall that evangelical Christians accept the Bible as the divinely inspired Word of God, and that it is our final authority and the supreme and only standard by which all human conduct is determined. Let us examine the following eight passages in view of light and heavy petting during courtship:

(1) "I plead with you to give your bodies to God. Let them be a living sacrifice, holy—the kind he can accept" (Rom. 12:1, TLB).

(2) "When you follow your own wrong inclinations your lives will produce these evil results: impure thoughts, eagerness for lustful pleasure" (Gal. 5:19, TLB).

(3) "Have nothing to do with sexual sin, impurity, lust and shameful desires. . . . God's terrible anger is upon those who do such things" (Col. 3:5–6, TLB).

(4) "For God wants you to be holy and pure, and to keep clear of all sexual sin so that each of you will marry in holiness and honor—not in lustful passion as the heathen do, in their ignorance of God and his ways" (1 Thess. 4:3–5, TLB). Phillips translates it: "God's plan is to make you holy, and that entails first of all a clean cut with sexual immorality. Every one of you should learn to control his body, keeping it pure and treating it with respect, and never regarding it as an instrument for self-gratification, as do pagans who have no knowledge of God."

(5) "Turn your back on the turbulent desire of youth and give your positive attention to goodness, faith, love and peace in company with all those who approach God in sincerity" (2 Tim. 2:22, Phillips). The Living Bible translates it: "Run from anything that gives you evil thoughts that young men often have, but stay close to anything that makes you want to do right."

(6) "But each one is tempted when he is carried away and enticed by his own lust. Then when lust has conceived, it gives birth to sin; and when sin is accomplished, it brings forth death" (James 1:14–15, NASB).

(7) "Do not give in to bodily passions, which are always at war against the soul. Your conduct among the heathen should be so good that when they accuse you of being evildoers, they will have to recognize your good deeds and so praise God on the Day of his coming" (1 Pet. 2:11–12, TEV).

(8) "Stop loving this evil world and all that it offers you, for when you love these things you show that you do not really love God; for all of these worldly things, these evil desires—the craze for sex, the ambition to buy everything that appeals to you, and the pride that comes from wealth and importance, these are not from God. They are from this evil world itself" (1 John 2:15–16, TLB).

To grasp the meaning of these passages written by Paul, James, Peter, and John, we need to understand that their first-century readers were new converts from paganism. The pagan cultures of New Testament times promoted and practiced sexual promiscuity as being religious, normal, and natural. Even their pagan gods were immoral. Pagan temples provided women, called priestesses, for sexual purposes. The sex act of a man with a priestess was an act of worshiping the pagan gods. For example, the temple of Aphrodite in Corinth had more than a thousand "sacred female slaves" who engaged in religious prostitution. The temples of Dionysius and Cabiri were both in Thessalonica. The new Christians were continuously exposed to the pressure of these and other sexual abuses, for in Greek life, a wife bore children to her husband and stayed at home to care for them. Her husband's social and sexual life, however, was with single women called *haitari,* who were educated and had an interest in art and literature. A Greek businessman or statesman did not hesitate to appear at a formal state banquet with his *haitari* at his side.

Make no mistake about it, the eight scriptural passages quoted above reject light and heavy petting as being wrong during courtship—in fact, in substance, and in principle.

But some critics resent any call for morality and insist on their right of moral freedom. Their demand for moral freedom is their first line of defense. To paraphrase Howard Hendricks, I like to answer this demand for freedom when I am on the twentieth floor of a skyscraper. There is an open window. We are all free to jump out that window. To my critics I say, "Go ahead and jump." You are perfectly free to do so. Be my guest. But once you are outside of the window, you are no longer free. You are immediately a slave locked within the prison of a dynamic law that dashes your helpless body against the pavement below. Yes, you are free to jump out the window, but you are not free to control the consequences of the jump. Yes, we are free to be sexually immoral, but we are not free to control the consequences of fornication.

The cynic asks, "What consequences?" I reply, premarital pregnancies, millions of abortions, venereal disease, illegitimate children, sexual disillusionment as a result of distrust and suspicion of the opposite sex, social ostracism of parents and offspring, and festering guilt feelings that linger through the years, blocking communication and marriage happiness—to name a few. All of these were in Paul's mind when he said, "Do not be deceived; God is not mocked, for whatever a man sows, this he will also reap. For the one who sows to his own flesh shall from the flesh reap corruption, but the one who sows to the Spirit shall from the Spirit reap eternal life" (Gal. 6:7–8).

We Christians cannot mock God and get away with it. The word "mocked" is a term of contempt meaning literally, "to turn up your nose." Paul is saying, "You cannot thumb your nose at God and get by with it." If a believer demands freedom to be immoral, he is responsible for that immorality and its consequences.

After Fornication, Then What?

Persons guilty of fornication know that the Bible calls it sinful in stern language. Some persons guilty of fornication seem to show no contrition or repentance, but in self-defense exhibit irrational, stubborn pride, all the while expecting and demanding forgiveness and acceptance from friends, the church, and community. Does not the Scripture teach that where there is no contrition and repentance, God remembers? (See Jer. 16:17; Hosea 7:2; 1 Cor. 5:11; Rev. 18:4–5.)

But this is no time or place to accuse. Although the Bible sternly condemns fornication as sinful, God's mercy and grace are in center court in the Scriptures. Fornication is a sin, but it is not an unpardonable sin, only one of many sins. How does a Christian receive forgiveness for fornication, for any sin, for that matter? In humble contrition one should, in unreserved submission, repent and ask God for forgiveness. Repentance involves contrition, a sincere change of heart and mind about sin, a turning from it, an about-face, and asking God for divine forgiveness. After repentance and a plea for God to forgive, God's forgiveness is instant and complete (Ps. 103:12; Isa. 1:18; Micah 7:19). When God forgives a person of fornication, *in God's sight, it is as if it had never happened.* Then that person must accept God's forgiveness. Since God has forgiven, then he or she must then forgive himself/herself. And any person aware of the problem should forgive and act as if it had never happened. Yes, some social consequences do remain, but divine forgiveness is a firm foundation upon which a normal, solid future can be built, as the one repenting follows Christ in a clean, moral life, and plans for what male and female are intended to be.

But let us not overlook the fact, as we have said, that *sex is good* within the marriage relationship according to the plan of the Creator. It is one of the most healthy and significant blessings the Creator gave us when he created us male and female. It is normal, it is Christian for courting couples to be concerned about sex, to seek wise counsel in trying to understand its place in their lives, and to have limited and controlled bodily contact during serious courtship. There should be no guilt feelings about this. To seek wise counsel in order to avoid the misuse and abuse of sex is a healthy sign. "He who sows to the Spirit will from the Spirit reap eternal life."

7

Live-in Relationships

The moral drift of our derelict culture has proceeded aimlessly until many voices are advocating that it is permissible for couples to live together before marriage. Some are tempted by this idea. In 1970 there were 523,000 known "unmarried couple" households in the United States. By 1978 this number had more than doubled to 1,100,000.[13] These figures do not include the thousands of clandestine live-in relationships. Some estimates maintain that these secret relationships could number three to ten million couples.

What are the moral implications involved in live-in relationships? I received the following letter, asking, "Why not?"

> My boyfriend (Ned) and I are contemplating living together for one or two years before considering marriage. We are intelligent, moral, law-abiding citizens. We love each other deeply. We want to live together, work together, to share, to trust and to love one another. We want to test marriage before moving blindly into it. We do not have financial means for marriage, and if we decide marriage isn't for us, we will just separate and avoid the heavy expense of divorce. Of what value is a piece of paper—the so-called marriage license, anyway? We are religious people, church members, and do not see any moral problems. Most broad-minded people think this will be the standard life style for the future. Some people who refuse to accept social change, including our parents, object to our plans. Why? (Mary)

Mary's letter states the usual arguments defending so-called trial marriages. I will respond to her letter by asking some pertinent questions: What is Mary and Ned's philosophy of life and system of values? Is Mary an object of his love, or his uncontrolled sexual drive? Is Ned's interest in Mary a convenience or a commitment? Does promiscuity promote real freedom or real bondage?

Mary says, "We want to love and trust one another." What is their definition of love and trust? Is it possible to have true love without commitment and responsibility? The Scriptures (KJV) tell us that love (charity) "suffereth long and is kind . . . vaunteth not itself . . . is not puffed up, doth not behave itself unseemly, seeketh not her own . . . thinketh no evil; Rejoiceth not in iniquity, but rejoiceth in the truth" (1 Cor. 13:4–6). When a couple insist on marriage on a trial basis, is this not evidence that they do not trust or love each other enough and do not really expect the marriage to succeed? Does not real trust mean that a couple has faith and confidence that they will succeed in marriage?

Aren't Ned and Mary assuming that sexual adjustment, once tested successfully outside of marriage, will be a permanent seventh heaven in marriage? Does a live-in relationship really test marriage? When a couple are not married, they are not married! How can marriage be tested in a state of singleness? It can't! Marriage is the institution whereby a man and a woman who love each other are joined together permanently in a special kind of spiritual, social, and legal dependence on each other for the purpose of becoming "one flesh" and the founding and maintaining of a family. Marriage can be tested only in a bona fide experience of marriage.

Nancy Stahl, in her column "Jelly Side Down," thinks that the real test for marriage is in a situation where the couple has two children with the flu, a semi-housebroken dog, a power failure during which eating and shaving must be done by candlelight, a drippy water faucet, storm windows being installed, bathroom ceiling being papered, the baby throwing up on the father's new suit, and an older child flushing a diaper down the toilet.[14]

Why don't we admit that a live-in relationship is not marriage?

It is immorality. It is fornication. Did not Jesus indicate his disapproval of the Samaritan woman who was living with a man who was not her husband (John 4:17–18)? What do religious people who are in a live-in relationship do with such Bible passages as "Because of the temptation to immorality, each man should have his own wife and each woman her own husband . . . " (1 Cor. 7:2), and "Finally then brethren, we request and exhort you in the Lord Jesus, that . . . you ought to walk and please God . . . For this is the will of God . . . that you abstain from sexual immorality; that each of you know how to possess his own vessel in sanctification and honor, not in lustful passion, like the Gentiles who do not know God . . . For God has not called us for uncleanness, but in holiness" (1 Thess. 4:1–7, NASB)? Note the word "immorality" in both passages is a translation of a form of the Greek *porneia* which means fornication. The King James translates it fornication. Thus, by claiming to be religious and yet demanding sex without marriage, Ned and Mary are displaying their ignorance of the Scriptures or they are willfully ignoring the Scriptures.

I am wondering how often the Marys and Neds of our society attend church? Do they have a daily devotional life, which includes prayer and reading of Scripture? Do they believe in supporting their churches through active service, tithes and offerings? What about social responsibility? The joy of social approval that a married couple has is lacking in a live-in relationship. Do the Neds and Marys realize what an awkward and embarrassing position they have thrust upon their parents, not to mention their brothers and sisters, their church, and their community? Do children really have a right to ask their parents to approve a life style that is immoral?

Sociologists point out that it is necessary for various social purposes for a society to know who is married to whom. We can see this truth in the practices of primitive societies. They did not have our neat set of county courthouse statistics, but they did put much emphasis on wedding ceremonies. It was a big occasion lasting for several days. All the community was invited. Thus for many years there would be those living who remembered who was married to whom.

Joanna Magda Polenz in her book *In Defense of Marriage* argues for the legal advantages of traditional marriage. She says:

> Such a marriage [live-in marriages] is harder to manage than a legal marriage. Ambivalence is present in everyone; we all have mixed emotions, which often provide suspicions and doubts about each other, feelings that are more apt to grow where there are no legal constraints on the relationship. We all tend to be more or less impulsive, so that we are apt to flirt, to be faithless, to put money into shaky investments, to do countless things that can cause deep emotional or practical damage to a love relationship. Legal liability helps to make us think ahead. Furthermore, many social facts of life make the legal bond useful. Why not use it? Why force children to suffer the slights that are always offered to people born illegitimately? Indeed, why not take all the psychological and social help the law provides? *A legal marriage is the best setting for an exclusive, permanent sexual relationship; it offers the most security and the most support, all of which may at some time be crucial* (italics mine).[15]

I would suggest that all those considering a live-in relationship come to grips with the facts that such relationships are caused by:

(1) self-centeredness, insecurity
(2) blind surrender to peer pressure
(3) a desire for the false freedom offered by the "new morality"
(4) the desire to appear unconventional, and
(5) rebellion against God, the family, society, and what male and female were meant to be.

8

Fantasy

Some may be tempted to resort to fantasy as they face the reality of their sexual drive. To understand fantasy, we need to distinguish between imagination, daydreaming, and fantasy. *Imagination* is a general term describing the power to form mental images of things, people, or situations. These images may involve past experiences or situations never experienced by the one imagining, or for that matter, anyone. Imagination generally does not involve evil ideas.

Daydreaming is a type of imagination, or dreaming while awake usually involving the fulfillment of a pleasant wish or need. Daydreaming is wrong when it is a copout and a flight from reality promoted by insecurity, lack of self-esteem, and fear. Daydreaming is good when it is directed by ambition, zeal, Christian values, and purposive goals.

Fantasy involves extravagant and deceptive daydreaming. It can include morally low thinking. It is the creation of mental images and ideas which are not real, and may not be moral. Perhaps we would all be surprised to know how much a Christian person through fantasy imagines intimate relations with a person who is not his/her spouse. Both single and married may practice such fantasy. I received a letter from a married couple stating that they had agreed that during their sexual experiences, in order to heighten their sexual intensity, they both would fantasize that they were having relations with someone else. In practicing this, they had been having some guilty feelings and wanted to know if this fantasy was wrong.

The main scripture on sexual fantasy is Jesus' statement from the Sermon on the Mount:

> You have heard that it was said "You shall not commit adultery." But I say unto you that every one who looks at a woman lustfully has already committed adultery with her in his heart (Matt. 5:27–28).

Adultery refers to an overt act. But Jesus here is expanding the Mosaic law to include inner moral purity. Note the words *every one!* He is saying every person, whether married or unmarried, who looks lustfully at any married or unmarried person of the opposite sex, is guilty of adultery. Jesus' words "Looks at . . . lustfully" are the key words in the passage. A lustful look is a sexual longing, wish, or desire toward another person. Jesus is saying that every person is guilty of adultery who, in fact or in imagination, sees a person of the opposite sex and wishes in fantasy that he could fulfill his sexual desires with that person, or decides to plan such a rendezvous. Jesus is saying that every person who does any of the above is as guilty as a married person who actually commits adultery. He is saying that a person's sexual sin begins at the point of his or her inner consent. He is saying that the lustful look is destructive to the lusting person and to future marriage. He is warning that the temptation to lust is strong and dangerous.

Lustful fantasy is not only a violation of the seventh commandment (Exod. 20:14), but it is a violation of part of the tenth commandment, "You shall not covet your neighbor's wife" (Exod. 20:17).

It is normal for husband and wife to have sexual longing and desire toward each other. This could take the form of fantasy when circumstances do not permit privacy. This is a good sign of a healthy, happy marriage. It is not lust! Lust always involves a fantasy attraction to someone other than one's own husband or wife.

Being human, we are all tempted to be attracted to and to fantasize about persons of the opposite sex. When a man sees a woman dressed in such a way that her clothing gives an inviting display of her body, he may easily entertain thoughts that could lead to lust. If a woman likes a man, and he touches her or puts his arm around her in a friendly but suggestive manner, it is easy for thoughts to arise in her mind that could lead to lust. Being human, it is very, very difficult for us to keep evil thoughts from coming into our minds. But these initial thoughts, in themselves, are not sinful and should not be labeled lustful. However, when a person willfully and deliberately accepts such thoughts, encourages them, entertains them, wishes the idea could become reality, and resolves to plan in that direction, he is sinning! He is lusting! He is committing adultery!

The Scriptures teach that no temptation is irresistible for a Christian. Paul warns us to be careful about temptation. He says:

> Therefore let any one who thinks that he stands take heed lest he fall. No temptation has overtaken you that is not common to man. God is faithful, and he will not let you be tempted beyond your strength, but with the temptation will also provide the way of escape, that you may be able to endure it (1 Cor. 10:12–13).

To avoid situations leading to sexual fantasy, Christian men and women, whether single or happily married, can still have friends of the opposite sex. But for a single person to meet regularly, alone, with a married man or woman, is to set up a situation that may be open to doubt and question. It could suggest that other dimensions may have replaced friendship. Such behavior amounts to provoking temptation. On the other hand, some people, both married and single, practice social isolation and hibernation. This is sad indeed! All people need friends, many friends. When a courtship or marriage rests upon Christian agape love, commitment, fidelity, and trust, there is little room for suspicion. Yet, Christians should control their friendships and keep them on the level of friendships.

Why do singles want to fantasize sexual relations? Could it be the result of false philosophies and value systems? Could it be a lack of knowledge about the true nature of Christian love? Could it be that such persons are self-centered and have never grown up emotionally?

Not only does illicit sexual fantasy violate the seventh and tenth commandments and the teachings of Jesus, but it is an easy step to other evil acts. Few would want the details of their fantasy to be known to everyone in the community. As a person thinks in his heart, so is he (Prov. 23:7, KJV). Thus, we are convinced, sexual fantasy is out of line with what male and female were intended to be.

9

Homosexuality

In recent years our culture has encouraged people to consider homosexuality as an alternative life style. Let us consider what homosexuality is and what the proper Christian attitude toward it should be. The word *homosexual* is a general term referring to sexual desire toward and sexual activities with a member of one's own sex. It includes both males with males and females with females. The word *lesbian* is a specific term referring to female homosexuals.

In the past, too many evangelical Christians have harbored fear and hostility toward homosexuals and have self-righteously turned against them. Most homosexuals want and need help; we Christians need to help them. We must change from an attitude of rejection to one of sympathy, empathy, understanding, and love. We are to *hate sinful patterns of behavior,* but we are to *love wayward persons* and take the initiative to help them. Followers of Christ must love and minister to all people with problems. This is the central thrust of the Scriptures. We, too, are only sinners saved by grace. Just as God loved us and saved us, he loves homosexuals and can save them, too.

We Christians are faced with a difficult dilemma, a choice between two ideas that seem to be in conflict: (1) the message of the Bible that we are to love and minister to all people in need and (2) the message of the Bible that homosexuality is sinful. We must keep a healthy balance between God's moral law and his divine forgiving grace. Since our culture does not give us a true picture of God's attitude toward homosexuality, it behooves us to make a careful study of what the Scriptures teach about it.

In our culture, homosexuality is promoted by liberal thinkers as an acceptable life style. The media gives it much free publicity. It has been dignified by the philosophy of humanism. The true picture of God's attitude toward sin and homosexuality is largely ignored and hidden from view. Since the Bible is our final authority, Christians want to know: *What does the sacred Scripture say about homosexuality? What is the defense used by homosexuals to justify it? How do Christians respond to that defense? What causes homosexuality? What hope is there for homosexuals?* We now turn our attention to these questions.

The Old Testament and Homosexuality

Genesis 1:28 ties human sexuality to procreation—reproducing after its kind. God said to Adam and Eve: "Be fruitful and multiply, and fill the earth and subdue it . . . have dominion over . . . every living thing that moves upon the earth." The fruit of an apple tree is apples. The fruit of mankind—husband and wife—is another human being. Thus, homosexuality cannot carry out the first command of God to the human race.

Genesis 2:24 ties human sexuality to a unitive relationship between persons of the opposite sex—husband and wife. "Therefore shall a man leave his father and his mother, and shall cleave unto his wife: and they shall be *one flesh*" (KJV, italics added). This one-flesh unity refers to the spiritual and bodily union of husband and wife in sexual intercourse. It is a profound, personal experience of physical, emotional, and spiritual pleasure between husband and wife. Jesus quoted this passage from Genesis as a foundation for his teachings about marriage (Matt. 19:4–5; Mark 10:7–8). It is obvious that the structural makeup of the physical bodies of two males or two females makes it impossible for them to experience this one-flesh unity. Thus, homosexuality is rejected by the creative and purposive plan of the Creator-God.

In the eighteenth chapter of Leviticus, we are given a list of divine commands designed to protect the sanctity of marriage and to maintain moral respect for the family as a divine institution. These Levitical laws are grounded in the Genesis order of creation. In the midst of this list condemning incest (verses 6ff), and adultery (verse 20), we are told, "You shall not lie with a male as with a woman; it is an abomination" (verse 22). The Living Bible translates it: "Homosexuality is absolutely forbidden, for it is an enormous sin." Following this list we read:

> Do not defile yourselves in any of these ways, for these are the things the heathen do; and because they do them I am going to cast them out from the land into which you are going. That entire country is defiled with this kind of activity; that is why I am punishing the people living there, and will throw them out of the land. You must strictly obey all of my laws and ordinances, and you must not do any of these abominable things; these laws apply both to you who are born in the nation of Israel and to foreigners living among you . . . For I am Jehovah your God (Lev. 18:24–26, 30,TLB).

The New Testament and Homosexuality

In the book of Romans, Paul's theme is that all people, both Jews and Gentiles, need salvation through faith in Jesus Christ. In Romans 1:18–3:20, he describes the wrath of God against the ungodliness of the Gentiles. Part of this ungodliness was the sin of defiling the human body. In condemning the defilement of the body, Paul singles out homosexuality. He explains that because of their ungodliness:

> Therefore God gave them up in the lusts of their hearts to impurity, to the dishonoring of their bodies among themselves, because they exchanged the truth about God for a lie and worshiped and served the creature rather than the Creator, who is blessed forever! For this reason God gave them up to dishonorable passions. Their women exchanged

> natural relations for unnatural, and the men likewise gave up natural relations with women and were consumed with passion for one another, men committing shameless acts with men and receiving in their own persons the due penalty for their error. And since they did not see fit to acknowledge God, God gave them up to a base mind and to improper conduct (Rom. 1:24–28).

Homosexuality was a common practice of the pagan world in New Testament days. The Greeks practiced male prostitution. The Romans copied it from the Greeks and "out-Greeked" the Greeks. The Roman Emperors, including Julius Caesar, Hadrian, and Trajan, entered into formal sexual contracts with male lovers. Such contracts were socially approved. The state derived revenue from widespread homosexuality. Paul utterly rebelled against it, denouncing it as ungodly (opposite God's holiness) and antisocial. In summary, he said that those who practice homosexuality are consumed with lust and passion. They are committing shameless acts, acts that are contrary to nature. They are immoral and wicked. They have depraved minds. Because of impure and defiled hearts they are dishonoring their own bodies. They have changed the truth of God into a lie and are worshiping themselves rather than God. They know that God has decreed that those who do such things deserve to die. Yet they not only approve of homosexuality but practice and promote it. Because of these sins, Paul thunders three times, "*God gave them up*" (Rom. 1:24, 26, 28, italics added). It is difficult to imagine a more direct, decisive, and scathing attack on homosexuality than these words of Paul.

In writing to the Corinthian Christians, Paul instructed them not to tolerate immorality among their Christian brothers: "Do not be deceived: Neither the sexually immoral nor idolaters nor adulterers nor male prostitutes nor homosexual offenders . . . will inherit the kingdom of God" (1 Cor. 6:9–10, NIV). In writing to Timothy, Paul associated homosexuality with the lawless, the disobedient, the ungodly, the unholy, the profane, and sinners (1 Tim. 1:8–10). There are four other Bible passages that indirectly associate homosexuality with sinful behavior (Gen. 19:4–9; Judg. 19:1–30; 2 Pet. 2:1–22; Jude 3–23).[16]

Although Jesus never spoke directly about homosexuality, his teachings on sexuality and marriage are definite, simple, and clear (Matt. 5:27–28; 19:3–12; Mark 10:2–9). Jesus did not do away with the Mosaic Law which dealt specifically with human sexuality; rather, he clarified and extended it to completeness and perfection (Matt. 5:17–18). For anyone to teach or imply that Jesus' teaching leaves room for a "sinless" homosexuality reflects irrational thinking and nonsense. Jesus' teachings are a clarion call to do battle against the misuse of sex in all its forms.

"The whole text of the Bible either celebrates sexuality as a positive gift from God, as in the Song of Solomon and Proverbs 5:15–23, or rejects aberrant sexuality without embarrassment, openly calling a spade a spade."[17]

The Cause of Homosexuality

What causes homosexuality? It is a habit learned through cultural experience. It is not inherited through the genes. It is a learned behavior. Its cause is basically and ultimately the result of the God-created free *human choice*. This choice of homosexuality is encouraged and promoted by the media, the strong human sexual need, and social situations that make it easy to initiate and develop homosexual experiences.

Some often make much of psychological conditioning in the family, such as a dominating mother or a neglecting father, as the cause of homosexuality. These conditions are present in thousands of homes and are influential in determining the bent of human behavior. But these conditions do not automatically cause homosexuality. They only tend to influence human behavior. The weakness of the argument lies in the fact that millions of boys and girls grow up in homes with a dominating mother or a neglecting father, or both, and do not become homosexuals. They choose to say *no* to evil.

Other social situations where there is no opportunity for association with the opposite sex, such as prison, some military situations, and so on, provide a climate for homosexual behavior. But millions of people in these situations have rejected homosexual opportunities. They have willfully said no and refused to start down the trail of an evil, empty life.

Evaluation of the Homosexual Movement

Homosexuals reject biblical authority and Christian ethical principles and use current cultural relativism and situation ethics as their guidelines. They are following the winding, drifting path of sinful, decaying culture. They use the immoral ideals of a sinful culture to judge the Bible rather than using biblical, moral ideals to judge culture. They disregard the authority of the Scriptures and are in rebellion against God, yet some of them pose as Christians. They reject moral law, yet insist on such laws as: (1) each individual is entitled to choose his own life style and (2) each individual has freedom as to his or her sexual preference.

Some homosexuals talk in beautiful language about the personal satisfaction of homosexual experiences and assume that homosexuality is Christian. Bishop Bennett J. Sims of Atlanta, Georgia refutes their assumption:

> In regard to the image of God it is crucial to any Christian understanding of sex that the divine image in humanity is incomplete without both man and woman, which is to hold that the aim of Christian sexuality is not personal satisfaction, but interpersonal completeness. "The two shall become one flesh" (see Genesis 2:24 and Mark 10:8). This is the ancient prescription. One plus one equals one: completeness. It remains a great mystery since human experience is imperfect, even in rapture. But from the mystery we can discern the meaning of the ideal of completeness, which is *the union of opposites,* or the coming together of differences. This does not mean simply genital differences (though this is fundamental to a biblical understanding of sexuality) but such differences as personality, temperament, social function, and

aspiration, all gathered into the physical symbol of genital differentiation.[18]

Bishop Sims' concept of interpersonal completeness, resting upon the biblical teaching of male and female created in the image of God, decisively rejects homosexuality as a distorted and perverted concept of the Creator-God's intentions for male and female. Homosexuality is incomplete, impotent, and sterile in promoting and producing "personality, temperament, social function, and aspiration," as well as sexual satisfaction.

The Defense of Homosexuality Examined

The three lines of reasoning pro-homosexuals use in defense of their case are as follows:

(1) Some homosexuals attempt to show that the Bible does not condemn homosexuality but actually approves it. This is done by selecting small half-truth proof texts and then twisting their meaning to suit a theory, by reading ultraradical ideas into passages taken out of context, and by ignoring the main thrust of the Scriptures concerning the holiness of God and evilness of sin. The following statements are examples of this distorted reasoning: "We are faithful to our companion. We do not commit adultery. We are moral persons." A careful examination of these half-truth proof texts is sufficient to see that the homosexual's ideas reflect the picture of a drowning man grasping at a straw. Evangelical Christians recoil in abject indignation at such distorted and perverted biblical interpretation.

(2) Some argue that homosexuality is constitutional: that is, it is a fixed life style in that it is inherited; it is genetic. Thus, the homosexual is not responsible for his homosexuality and cannot change, and therefore homosexuality cannot be sinful. Some homosexuals admit that the Bible does condemn active homosexuality but insist that it does not condemn constitutional homosexuality. I know of no biblical or scientific evidence to substantiate the assumption of constitutional homosexuality. There

are few psychologists or psychiatrists today who would advocate the idea that homosexuality is biologically inherited.

(3) Other homosexuals reason that homosexuality is not any worse morally than heterosexual adultery. This is true. But both are wrong! This thinking uses one sinful pattern of behavior to justify another. If our culture followed this reasoning, there would be a total breakdown in moral relationships, and civilization would collapse.

The saddest part about efforts to defend homosexuality is that some church leaders join in its defense. Richard F. Lovelace says:

> It has to be recognized that many advocates of active gay acceptance within the church are either gay themselves, or engaged in heterosexual activity outside marriage, and are motivated by the feeling that it is unfair for them to indulge in this behavior while denying it to homosexuals. Church leaders involved in this behavior are unwittingly reproducing the same kind of moral cancer which afflicted the church in the centuries before the Reformation.[13]

Why Is Homosexuality Sinful?

Homosexuality is a violation of the direct commandment of the Holy Scriptures. It is a violation of biblical principles flowing from the Scriptures as related to marriage. It is a violation of the purpose of God as revealed when he created male and female in his image. It is a violation of another person even among consenting adults. The effects and results of homosexuality on individuals and society are negative, unsocial, and immoral. If all persons everywhere adopted homosexual behavior, society would soon cease. Homosexuality is a mockery of God's beautiful design of male and female physical bodies and his intentions for them. It is a sick life style, an individual and social dead-end street.

Hope for Homosexuals

Homosexuality is not a mental disease, but, rather, it is a learned behavior. Therefore, it can be unlearned. God's love, mercy, and grace are available to all people who sin (Rom. 1:16). The leadership and resources of the Holy Spirit are available to all for the asking. The Bible plainly calls for repentance from sin. Jesus, Peter, and Paul all made repentance and faith the door to the kingdom of God. Repentance from sin and acceptance of Christ by faith bring spiritual victory. After repentance, faith, and victory in Christ, new Christians will want to follow Christ in every aspect of their lives including their sexual behavior. Being in the world, they must follow Christ and work to reflect Christ and his message to the sinful culture about them. They are in social interaction in the world, but they do not follow the evil practices of the world. Homosexuality has no future for the survival of the race. Any philosophy that turns its back on the future is a sick philosophy.

But *homosexuality is not an unpardonable sin nor the greatest sin.* (The greatest sin is the sin of rejecting God.) Homosexuals *can* change their sexual life style and be healed in Christ through repentance and faith. Paul listed homosexuality among the sins of the unrighteous people who would not inherit the kingdom of God (1 Cor. 6:9–10). Then he said to the Corinthian Christians, "*And these are just the characters some of you used to be. But now* you have washed yourselves clean, you have been consecrated, you are in right standing with God, by the name of the Lord Jesus Christ and by the Spirit of God" (1 Cor. 6:11, Williams, italics added). Some of the Corinthian Christians had been homosexuals following the pagan life style. But now, in Christ, their former life style was changed. Yes, there is hope. Such a life style can be changed, in Christ, today, to reflect what male and female were intended to be.

10

Sexual Self-Control

Never-married singles are concerned about their sex needs and drives. They are asking (and rightly so): What are we supposed to do with our sex drive? Is it possible for us to meet our sexual needs in ways that are in harmony with Scripture and are acceptable to God? The answer is a firm yes, but to do so involves a determination to follow divine Christian principles. Sexual self-control involves exercising restraint over one's own impulses, emotions, and desires. It includes avoiding anything that would lead one to break God's commandments, including fantasy.

There are some who seek to fulfill their sexual needs by watching television shows or movies with passionate love-making scenes, or by reading erotic novels and sex magazines. These do not have to be explicitly pornographic to cause problems. Although they may produce some feelings of sexual pleasure up to a point, such practices are actually self-defeating. Instead of satisfying sexual need, they arouse a desire for sexual intercourse which God created for marriage only. This is not to say, or even imply, that the sexual feelings and desires of a single person are sinful. But unless some positive steps toward control are taken, sexual needs can be very frustrating, and self-control can be very difficult. Only each individual knows what arouses him/her sexually. So the first step in self-control is to avoid that which one knows will stimulate him sexually. On a positive note, those who keep busy with creative activity, a challenging career, or altruistic service which absorb much of their attention and energies will have less difficulty with sexual self-control. The rule is *you control and direct sex. Don't let sex control and direct you.*

Self-release

Through the years many people have asked, "What about the possible option of masturbation as a means of self-control?" Let us examine this honest question. Since the term *masturbation* has carried many negative meanings traditionally, in recent years I have preferred to use the term *self-release*. Self-release refers to the stimulation of one's own genitals (penis or clitoris) by the hands and fingers for the purpose of achieving orgasm.

It is helpful to examine some historical developments related to masturbation. Following the industrial revolution, the humanistic writings of our secular culture freely promoted sexual promiscuity before and after marriage. They sanctioned masturbation, but orthodox Christianity took a dim view of it. In trying to counterattack the sexual promiscuity of the humanistic writings, orthodox Christianity went to the other extreme and embraced a strict moral sex code that approached asceticism; that is, the spirit is good and the flesh is evil. This extreme approach was the result of cultural conflict and not the application of scriptural principles. The pages of this history are filled with the warning of orthodox Christians that masturbation would cause poor health, brain damage, feeblemindedness, insanity, blindness, epilepsy, loss of sexual desire, and future sterility.

With the coming of industrialization, urbanization, and scientific progress in biology, sociology, and psychology, all these ideas have been shown to be false. Gradually, evangelical theological schools and churches made a more thorough study of the Bible and its relation to sex and marriage. They began to apply their Christian faith and commitment to all areas of life, including each person's sexual needs. Thus, we have had to rethink our concepts about self-release and label most of the old ideas as false.

We have been forced to replace them with ideas that are in line with Scripture, basic Christian principles, and the creative purposes of God in nature.

Today there is still a division among evangelicals about whether or not self-release is right or wrong. Some hold to the concept that "all self-release is sinful." A growing number of pastors, counselors, and Christian education leaders are saying that self-release is sinful under certain conditions but is not sinful under other conditions. But the question, "Is self-release right or wrong?" is still a very controversial moral question among evangelicals today, though seldom discussed openly.

Arguments Opposing Self-release

Those who say all self-release is sinful are generally conservative evangelicals. They are sincere, committed Christians, and for the most part are doctrinally sound in their theology. Many of them are educated. Let us examine their main arguments.

1. In the past, some have quoted Genesis 38:8–11 arguing that Onan was condemned for self-release. Actually Onan was not practicing self-release. He had sexual intercourse with Tamar but withdrew before orgasm to avoid making her pregnant. Onan was punished by God because he defied the Hebrew law which required him to marry his deceased brother's wife and produce offspring to carry on his brother's name.

2. Most conservatives admit that the Bible is silent on the subject of self-release but insist that it is a violation of the basic moral principles of the Scriptures. They say that when Paul exhorted the Ephesians that "Immorality and all impurity . . . must not even be named among you, as is fitting among saints" (Eph. 5:3), he included the sin of self-release. They say that when Paul advised Timothy to "Set the believers an example in purity" (1 Tim. 4:12) and to "Flee also youthful lusts" (2 Tim. 2:22, KJV), he included self-release. They read the idea that "all self-release is sinful" into many other passages, including 1 Corinthians 6:9, 18, and Ephesians 5:12. They claim that these passages are saying that one

cannot avoid lust and have a pure heart unless he avoids all sexual self-release.

This assumption is questionable. The context of all the above passages indicates the obvious misuse and abuse of sex—fornication, adultery, homosexuality, and bestiality. If God had thought that self-release was lustful and sinful, surely he would have stated so specifically in the Scriptures.

3. There are those who assume that it is impossible for a person to practice self-release without sexual fantasies involving sexual intercourse with someone other than one's spouse. In such a case, it would be a violation of Jesus' teaching: ''Everyone who looks at a woman lustfully has already committed adultery with her in his heart'' (Matt. 5:28). But this argument is questionable, as there is much evidence that persons *can* practice self-release without fantasizing sex with someone else. Of course, many do so fantasize, but many others will testify they do not.

4. Another argument used to oppose all self-release is that guilt feelings follow self-release. This argument is weak at three points. First, not everyone who practices self-release has guilt feelings. Second, it is the insistence that all self-release is evil that causes guilt feelings. Our conscience makes us feel guilty when we do something that we have been taught is wrong, but our conscience does not tell us what is right or wrong, apart from what we have been taught. Third, when it is explained to individuals that self-release *under the right conditions* is not sinful, guilt feelings disappear. Thousands will testify to this. Paul Tournier distinguishes between ''real'' guilt and ''false'' guilt. It is false guilt when a person feels guilty over self-release because he thinks that it is sinful or because he is afraid it will cause future sterility, feeble-mindedness, poor health, and so on. Real guilt follows when one violates God's instructions—the Ten Commandments, the teachings of Jesus, and so on.

5. In their criticism of all self-release as sinful, critics seem to be saying that most all thoughts about sex before marriage are evil. This idea is getting dangerously close to medieval asceticism. The Roman Catholic church has condemned all self-release as evil.

They say that "every genital act must be within the framework of marriage."[20] Evangelicals argue that fornication, adultery, and homosexuality are rejected by the dictates of both the realities of nature and of biblical revelation. But Catholics include self-release with fornication, adultery, and homosexuality. They admit that self-release is not rejected by the Scriptures but insist that it can be logically assumed from the basic principles of the Scriptures. Such an assumption can be rejected on two grounds: (1) God created the genitals so that self-release could be used as a means of self-control and (2) the concept of self-release as evil reflects ascetic teachings which are contrary to New Testament sexual ideas.

Scientific Evidence

Is there any other evidence in favor of self-release? There is a scientific principle that failure to exercise any part of the physical body will cause it gradually to decline and deteriorate. When people refuse to allow their God-created sexual system to be exercised through self-release over long periods of time, while considering and hoping for a good future marriage, that system will gradually be weakened and eventually rendered impotent. In discussing this subject, Robert N. Butler, M.D., and Myrna I. Lewis have said, "Total abstinence from sexual activity can be tension-producing and may result in impotence in men and loss of lubrication . . . in women."[21] Dr. Ed Wheat and Gaye Wheat, in discussing the sex life of married couples, state, "The maxim which applies best to sex after sixty is simply—*use it or lose it.*"[22]

Natural Evidence

God created nocturnal emissions for men—emissions of semen in sleep and in dreams. This can give some release. Men should lean heavily on sublimination—creativity (exercise, and so on) and nocturnal emissions. Many men do so. This restraint is good. But the cold fact remains that it is unrealistic to expect most men to depend completely on these means for sexual self-control until a future marriage. (When we meet a fact in the road, let us face it.) This is especially true of the formerly married.

Moral Evidence

The occasional practice of self-release for the purpose of self-control can reduce the temptation to fornication and adultery and save a person from sins clearly condemned in the Scriptures. Did not God create the potential of self-release? What do we suppose was his purpose? Would he create it, let it stand idle, and say it is sinful to use it?

A Defense of Limited Self-release for Men

Sex is major in all of our lives, and it is normal for those in the courtship years to think and plan toward their sexual future in marriage within the framework of biblical guidelines.

As I stated in my earlier book, *Sexual Understanding Before Marriage,* my position is that self-release is sinful for males *before* marriage

(1) when its sole motive is sheer biological pleasure unrelated to anything else,
(2) when one allows it to become a compulsive habit which controls his or her person, and
(3) when the habit results from feeling inferior and insecure and causes guilt feelings.[23]

On the other hand, I feel that self-release *can be right and is not sinful when it is a limited, temporary program of a man for the sole purpose of sexual self-control until marriage.* Today I still feel that if single men are fully committed to leading a clean, pure, spiritual, and moral life until marriage, occasional self-release for self-control is acceptable to relieve physical and psychological tension and therefore promote emotional well-being. So long as self-release does not become a compulsive habit or simply a means of gratifying lust, it is not immoral and may be thought of as being within the basic principles of the Scripture and the will of God. When the sole motive is self-control, it is a moral act. Self-release under the right circumstances is in harmony with the purpose God had in mind in creation when he gave us the blessing of sex.

Self-release for Women?

In my earlier book, *Sexual Understanding Before Marriage,* I opposed single young women practicing self-release on the ground of the inherent sexual differences between men and women. The biological nature of the female sex drive seemingly does not include as strong a biological demand for self-release as is true with males. This is especially true during the teen years. The male reaches his sexual peak in the late teens and his biological nature contains a strong demand for release. Females do not reach their sexual peak until approximately ten or twenty years later. The male has a gradual accumulation of seminal fluid that automatically stimulates him sexually and demands release. Females have nothing similar to this.

However, in recent years I have softened my feelings about women and self-release. There seems to be more evidence accumulating that single women have considerable pressure and need for sexual release. In men, pressure, due to the buildup of ripe sperm in the epididymus and the seminal vesicles, gives men a greater biological need for self-release than women. However, as women mature, they seem to be equal to men in psychological and emotional need for self-release. Many women say that there is a time during the menstrual cycle each month that they have a greater desire for sexual release than at other times. I still feel that young teenage girls have little need for sexual self-release. I like to think it brings a special blessing for a young girl marrying in the early twenties to achieve her first orgasm with her young husband soon after marriage. However, there seems to be sufficient justification for mature Christian unmarried women in their mid-twenties and beyond to practice self-release occasionally for the purpose of self-control and for physical and emotional well-being until marriage. However, like men, they should avoid self-release for pure physical pleasure, or for sex as an end-in-itself. Sex is not a toy to play with. It is a strong, vital part of God's creation in male and female for ultimate love expression and reproduction in marriage. However, women vary in the effectiveness of self-release in dealing with sexual tension. For some women, although physical tension is relieved, self-release heightens their sense of loneliness because, for them, their sex desire is triggered by a need for intimacy with a husband in marriage rather than a biological urge.

To date, some evangelicals have stuck their heads in the sand and by-passed this whole problem. Yet, there are thousands of mature single men and women who are hungry for sexual experience in marriage and are fully worthy of it. They have a right to some positive help through self-control until marriage. After all, they are people, whom God created with sexual capacity. God loves them! They love him! Their sexual and emotional needs are real, just like those of all other people.

Cautions About Self-release

Christians, who practice self-release as we have described it, should be fully committed to the principle of living a consecrated spiritual and moral life until marriage and beyond. In the process of occasional self-release, they should anchor their thinking on such biblical principles as: God created me with a strong sex drive (Gen. 1:27); God created me for marriage (Mark 10:6–8); and God expects me to control sexual passions until marriage (Rom. 6:12, 1 Cor. 9:5, Titus 1:15). Before or after self-release, these persons should breathe a prayer to God, such as "Thank You, Lord, for the wonderful blessing of life and sex. Help me to practice sexual self-control until marriage. May I never violate another person or Your will. If it is within Your will, help me to effect a good marriage." Yes, prayer and concern about our sexual patterns of behavior belong together (1 Cor. 7:5). But self-release is not for the purpose of training in advance for good sexual adjustment in marriage.

Good sexual adjustment results only from husband and wife learning together in marriage.

Conclusion

What, then, should the behavior pattern of mature singles be as they come to grips with their God-created sexual nature and needs? When I consider all the circumstances involved, I feel that a rigid condemnation of all self-release as sinful is rather arbitrary, is unrealistic, and is out of harmony with the creative plan of God. My experience in counseling indicates that some people seem to have a greater aversion toward masturbation than even adultery. This is unfortunate, indeed. This attitude is a cultural legacy out of the past with deep roots in ascetic ideas. It is not scriptural. Unfortunately, some very capable and sincere pastors, church staff members, and lay leaders are caught in this trap. We must avoid the philosophy (1) that men and women are made up of two natures, the spiritual and the physical, (2) that the spiritual and the physical are enemies, and (3) that the spiritual should be exalted whereas the physical is base, ignoble, and should be denied dignity and value. This is a pagan philosophy. In Judaeo-Christian philosophy the spiritual and the physical aspects of either a man or a woman cooperate together in one functioning unit, as a person, a self, a soul. The spiritual and the physical complement and supplement each other. To ask which is the most important, the spiritual or the physical, is like asking which is the most important, the right wing or the left wing of a bird or an airplane?

Thus, we conclude that the process of occasional self-release as a method of self-control and within the limitations of biblical principles is not sinful. Its divine purpose is self-control and the development and preservation of one's mental, emotional, and spiritual well-being, all of which are necessary for a healthy sex potential until a possible marriage. It is not a violation of a command from the Scriptures. It is not a violation of broad, basic Christian principles. No person has been violated. The motive of self-control is good, not evil. It encourages hope and builds for the years ahead. It is a part of planning to be what male and female were intended to be.

PART III

Creative Planning Toward a Good Marriage

11

Personal Growth

Careful attention to one's personal growth is basic in creative planning toward a good marriage. Only living things grow. The Dead Sea is dead because everything flows into it and nothing flows out. Spiritual, emotional, and moral growth are necessary for a satisfying, productive life and marriage. Some people are human dead seas because they are self-centered, greedy, and lustful egotists. They want many things from others to flow into their lives, but nothing from them flows out by way of human service. Stagnation, deterioration, perversion, and decay follow. Personal growth is a must for anyone seeking a satisfying Christian life and self-fulfillment. A special plus for single people is that personal growth will help draw a responsible marriage partner and help prepare one to be a responsible marriage partner. Let us examine personal attitudes, feelings, and motives as related to an individual's personal growth.

Growth in Commitment to God

The first, the basic, the most fundamental aspect of personal Christian growth is commitment to God as revealed in Jesus Christ through the Holy Scriptures. The redeemed Christian has had the veil of secular paganism and sin removed from his heart and mind and can now come face to face in fellowship with Christ the

Savior. This personal relationship with him can cause an individual to be "changed into his likeness from one degree of glory to another" (2 Cor. 3:18). By *continually concentrating* on Christ one steadily grows to be more and more like him. As Williams translates it, "We . . . are being transformed into likeness to Him, from one degree of splendor to another." This means that as we grow, we develop godliness, moral purity, knowledge, insight, self-control, consistency in commitment, brotherly affection, and love. To rise from one degree of splendor to another as Christians, we must resist evil and be firm in our Christian faith.

To grow in Christian commitment means that we must get rid of those things that hinder spiritual growth. The secular culture tempts us to be busy with many unnecessary things, things that have little or no relationship to Christ or his gospel. Many of these things may be good, but they seldom produce Christian fruit and values. To put the good ahead of the best is sin.

Growth in Relationships

The second most fundamental aspect of personal growth is growth in relationship with other people. When God created male and female, he created them with a basic need for friendship and fellowship with others. Ultimately this includes the need for intimacy with another person of the opposite sex, that is, a relationship in which one can feel free to relax, open up, reveal himself, and be himself.

Single people often ask, "What can I do about loneliness, especially on weekends? Why is it that loneliness is my number-one problem?" The reason is that God created male and female for fellowship with others. When God was in the process of creating man and woman in his image, he said, "It isn't good for man to be alone; I will make a companion for him, a helper suited to his needs" (Gen. 2:18, TLB). This means that God wants singles to experience personal association with the opposite sex.

Others may ask, "Why do some people get dates often and I seldom get a date? And when I get a date, it doesn't develop beyond the first date." It is possible for a woman not be asked again if she refuses sexual advances. A Christian would not want to continue dating such a person. However, the problem may be that some people never develop the fine art of social interaction. We all need to grow in relationship with others. Experience in relationships is a great teacher.

Stepping Stones to Satisfying Relationships

Some suggestions on how to develop more satisfying relationships are in order. Singles need to develop a variety of friends—both male and female, young and old, single and married, educated and uneducated. They need to learn to accept each person for who he is, what he is, and where he is.

In developing courtship relations with the opposite sex, one starts small and moves slowly, allowing some time to pass in order to give him or her a chance to think. Sometimes men begin by rushing a woman. Sometimes women are equally guilty. On the first date he brings her a dozen roses and takes her to an expensive and formal dinner at a plush hotel. In so doing, he sweeps her off her feet and possibly out of his life. Personal growth and intimacy do not explode full-blown on the first encounter. There is no such thing as love at first sight. Personal growth, love, and intimacy result from a gradual process of building relationships. In the beginning stages of courtship, it is not improper to have more than one person under consideration at the same time.

Singles need to seek relationships in which both can grow together. Each needs to make a contribution to the other. When either takes more than he gives, an unhealthy relationship develops. Kindness, gentleness, and honest compliments can strengthen a courtship relationship, as can open affirmation. Affirmation is the highlighting or pointing out of a strong trait or ability. The one receiving the compliment knows the affirmation to be truth and will feel good because a strength or ability has been noticed.

Hindrances to Developing Close Relationships

Some people have attitudes that may block them from growing in personal relationships. Some have a fear of being hurt or of being rejected. They may fear a repeat of some previous painful experience. Thus they follow familiar, easy, safe paths. They avoid risks or a spirit of adventure.

Others may lack the courage to break an undesirable relationship yet fear if they don't break the relationship, they may be trapped in a bad situation. Thus they tend to avoid all relationships.

Other single people are bashful, shy, timid, or suspicious. They may like a certain person and would like to develop a personal relationship with him/her, but their insecurity causes them to say, "Surely he (or she) won't like me." Thus faint hearts seldom win a fair lady or gentleman.

Those who have the Christian philosophy that sex belongs to marriage only, often fear that possible prospects may only be interested in sex. This problem can be met by expressing moral convictions kindly but firmly in the early courtship days.

Some people are afraid of marriage when they consider the current high divorce rate. This fear fails to recognize that divorces are largely the product of unchristian practices and that happy marriages result when husband and wife concentrate on continued commitment to divine principles in their marriage relationship.

Another barrier to developing close relationships is unrealistic expectations. In courtship, one partner may expect marriage quickly while the other may be only slightly interested. A gap in expectations brings disappointment, and frustrations are inevitable. Envy, anger, self-pity, bitterness, and depression may follow. When these are allowed to fester beneath the surface, a personality develops that may repel others. The gap between reality and expectation must be faced if one is to avoid feelings of rejection and bitter disappointment.

How to Avoid a Break in Relationships

Once a courtship relationship has developed, be careful not to be oversensitive. Don't take yourself too seriously. Don't wear your feelings on your sleeve. Don't analyze every situation and each remark. Take compliments at face value. Don't read other things into what people say. Some words or actions need to be ignored, especially if they happen only once. If lack of courtesy, slighting remarks, or put-down tactics occur repeatedly, explain calmly and kindly that these particular things bother you.

Be sure to separate yourself as a person from issues. If a friend disagrees with your point of view, do not take that to mean that he or she does not like you.

Develop a forgiving attitude. Forgiveness is not just an event. It is an attitude. It is the closing of a breach in a relationship and may help avoid a break in relationships. Of course, it doesn't change the facts but it does change your feelings about the facts. This may lead to a changing of the offending behavior.

Growth in Self-esteem

The third and final aspect of personal growth is growth in self-esteem. There is a bad and a good kind of pride. The kind of pride in which a person talks about oneself too much in an exaggerated sense of self-importance is rejected in the Scriptures as evil. Jesus spoke of the good kind of pride when he said to his disciples, "Love your neighbor as yourself" (Matt. 22:34–39). Although Jesus' emphasis in this context was on loving God and loving other people, he indicated that a person is to love himself/herself, too. One's self must not be isolated from God and others. When one sees that he must love God and others, it is obvious that he must love (have confidence in) self, too. This good kind of pride is best described as self-esteem, self-confidence, or self-worth. To love God and others, a person must have self-esteem, an inner feeling of self-confidence, and self-worth. Likewise, a proper relationship with God leads to an awareness of one's self-worth. Self-esteem is necessary for singles to draw acceptable prospects in courtship and to prepare for a stable marriage. It is crucial to a happy, fruitful Christian life, occupation, courtship, and marriage. It is crucial in personal growth.

To grow in self-esteem, we need to know how we develop our

self-concept, that is, what do we think and feel about our relationships with others and what do we think and feel about our own behavior. We need to ask, "How do we arrive at our self-concepts?" that is, "What is the process that goes on in our minds that relates us to other people?"

First, this process involves *my imagination of how I appear to other people*. How do other people see me? What do they see when they see me? Do they see a person tall or short, white or black, slim or obese, educated or uneducated, accepted and loved, or unaccepted and rejected?

Second, the process involves asking myself, "*How do other people interpret what they see when they see me?*" How do they evaluate me? What do they think about me? Do they judge and label me after what they see of me as being good or bad, lovely or ugly, charming or grouchy, happy or sad?

Third, on the basis of what *I think* they see and how *I think* they evaluate me, *I form feelings about myself* such as pride or embarrassment, pleasure or depression, flattery or dejection, acceptance or rejection.

Note that it is *what we think other people think* about us that determines our self-concept. Our poor self-concept largely results from imagined criticism others make about us which we internalize and turn against ourselves. Note that the things we think others think about us are often untrue, so that our poor self-concept often rests upon a false foundation. Thus many of us go around carrying a picture of self in our mind that is a dim, dull, distorted likeness of our real self and our real potential. We show this picture to the people around us and use it to undersell ourselves to others and to ourselves.

The Behavior of Poor Self-Esteem

How do people with a lack of self-esteem act? They express themselves in many and varied ways, often opposite ways. Some avoid competition and isolate themselves from many community activities. Others are often overly critical of other people. Sometimes this critical attitude seems to be an effort to punish people for doing well what they themselves would like to do and are afraid to do. Others brag about themselves. They grab the conversation, run with it, and give themselves many "lefthanded" compliments. This behavior is an open effort to impress other people and thereby cover up their inner lack of self-esteem. Others, instead of complimenting themselves, direct the conversation in such a way that they force friends and associates to praise and honor them. When we have to use a "cork-screw" to pull a compliment out of a friend, it is not a compliment. A compliment is an unexpected surprise that is totally initiated by another person.

Other people who lack self-esteem worry about little things they have said or done, or that other people have said or done. Still others become extreme perfectionists in order to prove to friends that they are good at something. Sometimes a lack of self-esteem causes people to carry a chip on their shoulders. They become very sensitive, very jealous, and are easily offended. Lack of self-esteem causes others to become very pessimistic. They tend to believe the worst about themselves, about others, and about the future. In their fear they become distrustful of everyone.

The person lacking self-esteem craves affection, love, and understanding without realizing that he himself does not try to love or understand others. Thus, he tends to become a "dead sea" with everything flowing in and nothing flowing out. This promotes idleness, restlessness, daydreaming, frustrations, anxiety, and misery. It blocks spiritual, social, and intellectual growth in one's personality. If we permit it, these little molehills of insecurity can grow into neurotic mountains.

How to Develop Self-esteem

How can we develop our self-esteem to the healthiest possible level? The following four lines of action should be helpful.

We must admit our lack of self-esteem to ourselves. We need to practice introspection, that is, take a journey inward to examine our own inner attitudes and feelings. We need to go into a private room, lock the door, stand aside, and watch ourselves pass by. We need to study our inner attitudes and feelings thoroughly, accept the reality existing there, and respond to it. In other words, each person must admit to himself his lack of self-confidence, admit that he is afraid and that this has paralyzed his personal growth and left him helpless. He needs to admit that his problem is not his friends or his enemies. He is his own problem. To paraphrase the cartoon character Pogo, he needs to say, "I have met the enemy, and I am it." To take this step realistically is perhaps half the victory in developing self-esteem.

The second step is to admit that lack of self-esteem is not only self-destroying, it is actually a form of sin—a disease of the personality. The Bible tells us that sin is an inward condition of the heart. Thus the person must realize that he needs something that will reverse his fear of life, something that will jar him out of his apathy.

The third step involves making a change from being an inflowing Dead Sea to an outflowing Niagara Falls. This change is so great that a person must have direct help from God. It is impossible to cure insecurity by pulling ourselves up by our own bootstraps. A counselor or psychotherapist can help, but even they have their limitations. If a person is a Christian and has been following Jesus afar off, there must be a full rededication of self to Christ to change one's inner self from "inflowing" to "outflowing." If one is not a believer and wants to be, he must surrender his life to him who said, "I am the way, and the truth, and the life; no one comes to the Father, but by me" (John 14:6). The Scriptures say, "As many (unbelievers) as received him, to them gave he power to become the sons of God, even to them that believe on his name" (John 1:12, KJV). In humble sincerity, the person who has been an unbeliever and now wants to become a Christian should pray this simple prayer:

> Lord, I want to become a Christian. I now open the door of my heart and life and receive You as my Savior and Lord. I thank You for forgiving all my sins. Take control of my life from today forward. Lead me by Your Holy Spirit to be the kind of person You want me to be.

In simple language, this is a biblical description of how the new birth takes place.

Jesus' cross was an outflowing of his life to reverse our inflowing life to an outflowing life. To my knowledge, there is no other alternative to cure lack of self-esteem. This reversal is no hocus-pocus! It has been reality for millions.

There is a fourth and final step to strengthen our self-esteem. Since our "inflowing insecurity" has in Christ been reversed to "outflowing concern," we now need to devote ourselves to a program of planned Christian service, an outflowing life of activities, love, and understanding. It is the nature of a Christian to devote his life to people and projects outside himself. Tennyson, in *Locksley Hall,* spoke well when he said, "I myself must mix with action, lest I wither with despair." Through action, one's confidence, security, and happiness will grow from "splendor to splendor," and bear fruit. Only thus can one conquer his inner fears. As one looks to the future, he should be prepared for some failures, but he must also be prepared for and rejoice in small victories. One must learn to profit by each mistake and remember that there is no fear in an outflowing love, but outflowing love casts out all fear (1 John 4:18).

When singles, in their journey outward from insecurity, turn to Jesus Christ for security and put his teachings and principles into practice, they will not only grow personally, but they will voluntarily and spontaneously become concerned about others' needs and rights. We may be sure that this outflowing Christian life style will be an asset in attracting would-be suitors, and if followed by marriage, will tend to produce a fruitful and happy marriage.

12

Personal Appearance

Most people are attracted to the personal appearance of a prospective marriage partner and give secondary consideration to his/her inner qualities. This may be unfortunate, but we still need to give attention to that which may affect one's personal appearance—proper dress, nutrition, and exercise. When these are disregarded, one's opportunity for marriage may be adversely affected.

Dress

Since the Creator created men by nature to be more easily aroused sexually by visual stimuli than are women, there is a temptation for women to dress to get the attention of men through "sexy" appearance. Thus, a discussion of modesty in dress needs to be directed largely toward women. This is not to release men from the responsibility of proper dress. Nor does the fact that some women dress unacceptably justify men's unacceptable behavior toward them.

The word *modesty* as related to the display of the physical body has been rejected by our present, permissive culture as being out of date. Situation ethics and moral relativism, with their overemphasis on freedom and sex, have cut the foundation from under human modesty in America. Thousands of church members have ceased resisting and have surrendered to a cultural avalanche of immodesty. There has been a thundering silence coming from the Christian community. It was Abraham Lincoln who said, "To sin by silence when we should protest makes cowards of us all." To protest against immodesty in our culture often means to swim against the current and to be labeled a prude.

What does the Bible have to say about dress? In the Sermon on the Mount, Jesus warns us against allowing *things* to rule our lives. He said for us not to be anxious about what we wear. To worry about clothes does not add one day to the span of life. Striving for material things takes our minds off God and reflects a lack of faith in him (Matt. 6:25–33).

Paul, in discussing proper conduct in public worship, warned women against the elaborate and expensive fashions of the Gentiles (pagans) and called for modest and sensible wearing apparel (1 Tim. 2:9). In like manner, Peter warned women not to be concerned about external beauty through the display of elaborate clothing, expensive jewelry, and outlandish hairdos. Such excessive decorations were characteristic of the immoral pagans of that day. Instead he urged women to develop inner qualities of the heart, including Christian charm, grace, and a spirit that is quiet, gentle, and precious in God's sight (1 Pet. 3:3–4).

Modest adornment reflects inner character, maturity, and self-confidence. Some women, who otherwise seem to be fine Christians, dress and behave in ways which seem designed to excite and provoke men sexually. This behavior includes the wearing of plunging necklines, rising hemlines, split skirts, bare midriffs, tight sweaters, and shorts that present an open invitation, especially while walking or sitting. Due to greed for greater economic gain, the fashion industry keeps changing dress designs—first tight, then loose, hemlines up, then down, belts up, then down, in yo-yo fashion, ad infinitum, ad nauseum. When women frantically follow these erratic maneuvers, they appear to be making a pathetic effort to regain in outward appearance what they lack inwardly.

However, we must not push this idea too far, as some have, and insist that a Christian woman should wear only drab, sloppy clothing. Clothing should give protection, reflect decency, promote loveliness in appearance and grace in walking, sitting, or rising, without unduly calling attention to self. No one should dress in a way that tempts others to sin. Women who go to extremes to display their bodies through elaborate clothing (or the lack of it), gaudy jewelry, and excessive makeup are simply parading publicly their inner emotional problems, such as immaturity, insecurity, and lack of self-confidence and self-esteem.

It is impossible to set a single standard of modesty that would apply to all social situations. Clothing should enhance the individual's personality and body characteristics so that others are conscious of the person rather than the clothes. Women (and men) should be concerned about their inner character, spiritual maturity, and self-confidence and allow these qualities to be reflected through their outer adornment. Clothing designed to arouse and lure the opposite sex is unacceptable. However, in marriage, intimate garments in the privacy between husband and wife are both proper and beautiful.

People should not regard clothing as an end in itself. Rather, clothing should be a means to other ends—positive effects on self, other persons, and the kingdom of God. Clothing should be comfortable and enhance natural beauty so that people think on that which is good, pure, and lovely (Phil. 4:8).

Nutrition

As important as proper dress is, the health and vitality of one's physical body is even more important. It is useless for anyone to be overly concerned about inherited characteristics such as being too tall or too short, having big ears, a long nose, a scrawny neck, big feet, early baldness, or anything that cannot be changed. No one has a perfect body. People will accept us as we are if we are able to accept ourselves. However, if our physical shortcomings can be overcome with more attractive hairdos or clothing that minimizes irregular body shape, by all means let us do something about it!

Perhaps the most common problem related to personal appearance that can be remedied through sheer determination is being overweight.

Charlie Shedd tells us that if we weigh ten percent more than we should, we are overweight. If we weigh twenty percent more than we should, we are obese.[24] My research indicates that obesity in both men and women can hinder their chances of marriage.

Excess weight is often blamed on glandular problems. Actually only a few people have glandular problems which lead to overweight. Overweight is rarely, if at all, inherited through the genes. Body build is not a decisive factor. We need to understand and admit to ourselves that most obesity is the result of *eating too much, eating the wrong kind of food,* and *exercising too little.* It is as simple as that. The problem may be brought on by family eating habits, including an improper diet during childhood and youth.

Why do people overeat? It is often a habit that has slowly developed over a period of years. Some people eat to pass the time. Others eat to get their minds off personal problems. Some overeat in an attempt to satisfy unmet emotional and physical needs.

The National Institute of Health states that "A number of serious physical disorders can stem from, or be exaggerated by . . . overweight. These include hypertension (high blood pressure), premature heart attack, gallbladder and liver disease, osteoarthritis (from the pressure of excess pounds on the weight-bearing joints), emergence of latent diabetes, varicose veins, and a host of other conditions which can subtract years from a normal life span."[25] In addition, obesity adversely affects an individual's personality and emotional maturity. Obese people often pretend to be jolly, but in reality many are insecure and lonely, and may have guilt feelings and a lack of self-esteem.

What does the Bible say about our eating habits? We are told that what we eat has little or no connection with one's spiritual life (Mark 7:18–19; Acts 10:12–15; Heb. 13:9). Spiritual values come through God's grace and man's faith. However, the Scriptures do reject and forbid a life style that leads to excessive eating and consequent overweight. The book of Proverbs advocates that one's life style should include self-control at the table and warns of the danger of gluttony (Prov. 23:21).

In criticizing the Antinomians, Paul, who emphasized freedom and liberty, said that they gloried in their gluttony and drunkenness; their stomachs were their gods and therefore they were the enemies of the cross (Phil. 3:18–19). In his letter to the Corinthians, Paul said that our bodies are the dwelling place of the Holy Spirit. They do not belong to us; they belong to God. Therefore we should use every part of our bodies to glorify God (1 Cor. 6:19–20). Thus, an overemphasis on satisfying one's appetite for food amounts to worshiping an idol—putting one's stomach before the kingdom of God.

Although the Scriptures do not give us every detail about what to eat and not to eat, scientific nutrition does. Through years of painstaking research, we know much about the relation of food to health. These nutritional scientists have simply observed through research the guidelines and facts that the eternal God placed in human life when he created them male and female. Thus, indirectly, through the scientific study of nutrition, we have the Creator's details for physical health.

The following positive suggestions based on scientific research in nutrition should be helpful. Each day our diet should include each of the following types of food:

(1) Vegetables, green and yellow (uncooked when possible), such as beets, cabbage, carrots, celery, corn, spinach, lettuce, beans, peas, potatoes, and so on.

(2) Fruits (uncooked when possible) such as bananas, apples, oranges, grapefruit, pears, peaches, and so on.

(3) Meat—beef, fish, poultry, and so on. The meat should be boiled, baked, or broiled.

(4) Dairy products including skim milk, cheese, butter, and so on.

(5) Grain or seeds such as whole wheat, wheat germ, rice, oats, nuts, sunflower seeds, and so on.

Negatively speaking, we should avoid the following: Animal fat and all types of food cooked or fried in grease, and foods composed largely of starch (carbohydrates) or which are also heavy with rich fat-producing calories and largely empty of nutritional value, such as cakes, pies, desserts, macaroni, spaghetti dishes, and so on. Also, avoid processed foods purchased at the supermarket which usually have excess sugar and salt, and questionable nutritional value. In short, excess sugar, fat, and salt are the principal demons of good nutrition. All three lead to overweight.

Do not attempt to lose weight through fancy crash diets. Do not skip meals to lose weight. Eat regular meals. Avoid the diet fads involving various ratios of proteins, fat, and carbohydrates sold at drug stores. People who want to lose weight should *always* seek the guidance of the family doctor. People who are obese, once they have decided to lose weight, often resort to crash diets so they can get the pain of dieting over more quickly. But because they have not changed their eating habits, they soon gain back what they lost. Permanent weight loss comes slowly and remains off if one changes faulty diet patterns and eats sensibly.

But we must not assume that it is easy for an obese person to lose weight. When a person has been overweight many years, it may be difficult for him to change life-habits and self-concepts. He probably has mental images about himself which may or may not be true, but they are real. Thus he may need professional psychological help to lose weight and to keep weight down. Usually, when a person loses weight following a physican's instructions, he feels better about himself.

However, if after losing weight a person still feels fat, he should surely seek professional help. This is a psychological problem known as *anorexia nervosa,* in which a person may literally starve to death if he does not receive professional help.

To best meet the demands of our body, we should eat breakfast like a king (a large nutritious breakfast), the noon meal like a prince (an average meal), and the evening meal like a pauper (a small meal). To eat thus will help one to lose weight. To reverse the process, as is done in our sophisticated society, will cause one to gain weight on the same amount of food.[26]

Healthful eating habits will improve the functional capacity of our heart, lungs, and muscles and help us to live at our optimum physical capacity, a desirable conditioning which is our Christian responsibility. A welcome by-product is that proper eating will contribute more to the beauty of the skin and hair than expensive cosmetics and hair conditioners.

Exercise

In addition to good judgment in dress and careful nutrition, a thorough program of physical exercise is also important in maintaining good personal appearance. Many Americans get little exercise at work or during leisure hours. They ride in cars or buses rather than walk, use elevators instead of stairs, and sit at home, often glued to the television, instead of being physically active.

The U.S. Department of Health and Human Services tells us that regular exercise helps us cope with stress, improves our self-image, increases resistance to fatigue, helps counter anxiety and depression, tones muscles and burns off calories. Authorities recommend brisk, continuous exercise from twenty-five to forty minutes at least three times per week. However, the length of time of exercise should be determined by age and the intensity of the exercise. To exercise and condition the heart and lungs, they recommend cross-country running, jogging, swimming, stationary cycling, bicycling, handball, racquetball, tennis (singles), walking, and so on.

They question baseball, football, golf (on foot or by cart), softball, and volleyball as failing to meet the body's need for regular, vigorous, sustained exercise.[27] Of course, these activites are enjoyable, and help relieve tension. But they do not adequately strengthen and condition the heart and lungs or burn off many calories. The exercise we need does not require special athletic ability. Single persons, especially older singles, should plan their exercise program with the guidance of their personal physician. Excellent help can be had from the high school, college, or county health department.

A proper program of regular exercise is important in maintaining good personal appearance. It leads to graceful bodily movements, zest for living, and other attractive attributes. It often throws singles into contact with other singles in a situation that could lead to friendship and possibly marriage. Our nephew, while doing his internship for his M.D. degree, met his future wife on a racquetball court. One of our close friends, a college sociology professor, met her future husband while jogging on the high school track in her home community.

13

Qualities to Look for in a Marriage Partner

What qualities should a person look for in a future wife or husband? The marriage decision is the second most important decision of life, and should be carefully made following wise guidelines anchored in biblical principles, led by the Holy Spirit, and bathed in prayer. At the same time, it is a decision that each individual must make on his or her own, directed by reason, intelligence, and common sense. The decision should not be based on one aspect of life such as education, social status, economic security or physical beauty. The decision should be within the will of God, should include a personal commitment to marriage for life, should provide opportunity for Christian witness and fellowship, and should stimulate personal growth together.

It is difficult for a couple who have little in common to have a happy marriage. Trying to build a bridge over such a treacherous chasm can easily ruin a relationship. Avoid reading qualities into a person that are not there. Also avoid trying to change a prospect until he or she has the qualities of your liking, or trying to create qualities that are not there. Such an endeavor is likely to endanger a relationship, if not lead to an unhappy marriage. On the other hand, do not sit back and wait for the miracle of a perfect partner. Happy marriages are made by two imperfect people who may not see eye to eye on everything. Christian love and maturity can bring understanding and empathy. Yet, the more characteristics a couple have in common, the better are their chances of a successful marriage.

Let us examine some qualities to look for in a marriage partner.

1. The first quality to look for, always, is the philosophy of life—the beliefs, and the values of a prospective partner. What does he or she think about God? the Bible? the church? the nature and purpose of life? How important are persons, all persons in his/her system of values? Does he/she believe in freedom and justice for all or just for self? When there is a major ideological gulf between persons before marriage, it tends to widen between them after marriage until it affects other personal areas of their marriage. Granted, there may be some exceptions.

2. To be more specific, the person one marries should be a believing Christian. He or she, individually, should have received Christ (John 1:12) through personal repentance from sin (Ps. 34:18; Mark 2:17; Luke 5:31; 24:47) and faith in him as Savior and Lord (John 20:29; Eph. 2:8–9; Rom. 1:17), and should be active in the ongoing work of the body of Christ (Matt. 25:40; Mark 9:35; Rom. 12:11; Eph. 6:7). Such a person is generally guided by agape love and would have the capacity to understand and give spiritual, emotional, and economic support in meeting the needs of a marriage partner.

3. In the early stages of courtship, one should consider his friend's family background. Are this friend's parents happily married? Has he or she had a happy childhood? Have parents been *overindulgent* and *permissive*, that is, have they followed the false philosophy that love means absolute freedom with no discipline, no guidelines, no guidance? Some parents seem to think that if they give their children an abundance of material things, their children will automatically become mature adults. Or, have parents been *authoritarian* tyrants who refused to allow their child any freedom? Or have parents followed *a middle ground, walking the thin line between permissiveness and domination*, a line that reflects authority and leadership saturated with love and understanding?

One may be certain that any prospect's habits and life will reflect parents and childhood background. This is not to imply that a person who was reared in a permissive or authoritarian home would always fail in marriage or that one reared in a home characterized by Christian leadership and love would always succeed. A born-again Christian experience can reverse a life. Sometimes a person reared in an unhappy home is determined not to follow the philosophy of his/her upbringing. Also, some youth brought up in ideal family life do go astray. But a safe rule of thumb is that happy parents and a happy childhood are usually followed by a happy life and marriage.

4. What experience has this marriage prospect had in family life? What experience has he or she had in managing a household? In caring for children? Does he/she know the basic emotional needs of children and have some idea about how to meet them? After all, marriage involves household responsibilities and probably children.

5. How much work experience has a possible prospect had? Has he or she ever been gainfully employed? Was it for only one week or for a period of months or years? Could he or she receive a recommendation from the last employer? Has your friend had one or more years of being completely responsible for self-support?

6. Has your suitor's life reflected financial integrity and responsibility? Does he or she have a savings account? How much debt does he or she have now? Are there responsible plans for financial marriage responsibilities? Is he/she able to live within available income?

7. What type of personality does the person who entreats your love have in social interaction? Is he or she an extreme introvert or extreme extrovert? The former is an object for prayer, the latter a candidate for hanging! Either may be prisoner of his/her own insecurity and lack of self-esteem. Be careful about the person who avoids group relationships and lives in social isolation—a lonely, emotional hermit, who, in fear, wallows in a few narrow ideas and who rejects and is critical of the mainstream of life. He/she is not a good marriage prospect.

8. You need to consider whether or not your prospective partner has a sense of humor. One of our greatest human qualities is the blessing of laughter. It can bring a pleasant release of emotional energy varying from a smile or chuckle of simple amusement to a hilarious explosion. Laughter inspires relaxation, joy, and happiness. It can defuse a tense situation. To enjoy laughter is an index to one's own inner nature. To be able to laugh at self is an even better index. A good sense of humor adds spice to a marriage relationship.

9. It is important that prospective marriage partners be as near the same educational level as possible. I remember a young bride and groom who enrolled in college at age twenty. She worked while he got his B.A. degree in three years and three summers. Then he worked while she got her B.A. in the next three years. I like that spirit. When a wife or a husband drops out of the educational process, it is easy for an intellectual and cultural chasm to develop between them. Pleasant communication and understanding gradually decline. This does not mean that a wife and husband must have identical educational levels. If a wife or husband has less formal education than does the spouse, he or she must make an extra effort to keep informed to facilitate communication and pleasurable emotional response in her/his marriage. When educational experiences are at different extremes, it is easy for a marriage to be invaded by individualism.

10. Since our God-created sexuality is a major drive in all of our lives, singles need to consider the sexual attitudes of prospective partners. They would do well to avoid two extremes: (1) those playboy characters who seem to think sex is the only thing in life of value, and act accordingly, and (2) those who are afraid of sex and refuse to discuss it or think about it. In our culture, there is far more of the former than the latter and both should be suspect. A prospective marriage partner should have a positive philosophy about sexual self-control, should practice it in his/her relationships with you and everyone else, should show you personal respect and consideration, and should, at the proper time and place, be willing

to discuss with you attitudes and feelings about sex in marriage with calm frankness, without too much timidity and apprehension.

11. Sometimes physical beauty is the first and only quality some consider for marriage. This is especially true of men. Physical beauty *is a plus,* but it should *never* be the first quality to look for. It should ultimately have the last and least consideration.

Guys and gals should not back off from a person because he or she appears physically unattractive at first. Often when one comes to know the real, plain Jane or ordinary Jim, he or she will become physically attractive. The bottom line is that the first and final characteristics to look for are the inner personality qualities of the mind, heart, and soul—beliefs, values, attitudes, and motives plus sincerity, humility, gentleness, grace, and charm.

12. What is the attitude of a prospective marriage partner toward the nature of marriage? Does he/she consider it God-instituted and therefore sacred? Is it considered a total relationship, a life commitment, a permanent relationship? Is it a relationship of integrity and fidelity? Does he or she realize that there may be many inherent causes of tension and conflict in marriage? That there will be some conflicts? That in marriage both husband and wife must often choose between marriage and their individual selfish choices? That the marriage must always have first priority? A person must ask, am I marrying because of what this person can do for me? Or because of what I can do for him or her? Does he or she understand that the engagement commitment and the marriage vows do not automatically produce a good marriage? That a good marriage involves work—hard work, and new commitments daily?

A Christian attitude for a man toward his fiancée should be: "I consider that my major life assignment is to create a home in which my wife-to-be can become all that God intended her to be. As she develops that potential, then I will be fulfilled."

A Christian attitude for a woman toward her fiancé should be: "I consider that my major life assignment is to create a home in which my husband-to-be can become all that God intended him to be. As he develops that potential, then I will be fulfilled."

Married life and love is a two-way street. The husband gives himself to meet his wife's needs. The wife gives herself to meet her husband's needs. In this process both feel loved, feel secure, and the needs of both are fully met. There is no other alternative to a happy marriage. Christian agape love is necessary for a marriage to become all that God intended male and female to be.

14

Taking the Initiative in Finding a Marriage Partner

Our research indicates that 78 percent of never-married men and women would consider marriage for themselves now. Much of the evidence reveals that a high percentage of them would not only consider a good marriage but are anxious for and dream about it. Yet our research indicates that some Christian singles think it is wrong and unchristian to take the initiative in trying to find a marriage partner. Instead, they often sit down with folded hands and wait for God, or fate, or some coincidence to bring them a good marriage. Women are perhaps more prone to this attitude than are men. This attitude is unfortunate. It tends to delay and obstruct progress toward marriage.

Approximately 75 percent of the women and 60 percent of the men in our research sample were actively involved in the life of their church. Some active Christian singles have an extreme view of predestination. This belief can color attitudes on courtship and keep them from taking the initiative in courtship. For example, in response to the questionnaire, one wrote, "I feel if God wants me to meet someone, and marry, I will. If not, I'll live each day as it comes." Another said, "I don't worry about being single. If you are meant to marry, you will."

The importance of trusting God to lead in every area of our lives, including courtship and marriage, cannot be overestimated. It is imperative! But we fear that the above responses reflect the futile philosophy of fatalism—that is, the belief that events are fixed in advance for all time in such a manner that people are powerless to change them. It makes personal puppets on strings with God pulling the strings. It rejects the biblical concept of the freedom of man.

If a never-married Christian single wants to buy a house, it is normal to trust God and pray for the leadership of the Holy Spirit. But does he then sit down and wait for God to deliver the house to him? No! He takes the initiative. He searches diligently. He counts the cost (Luke 14:28). In all of life's problems and decisions, we need to keep a healthy balance between (1) the sovereignty of God, his will, and (2) the freedom of man to think, to will, to act. As Christians, we all need to trust God as though everything depends on him and work as if everything depends on us. Yes, it is normal, it is Christian, we believe, for the never-married, who feel that God created them for marriage, to take the initiative in their quest for a good marriage. They will hold on to God in faith, and, at the same time, work in searching for a good marriage in a systematic manner characterized by wisdom, dignity, courage, and determination. They should leave no stone unturned in the search. They should be assertive without appearing too forward or brash in self-confidence. The search should be bathed with prayer and with persistence.

The reader may be asking, "Should women take the initiative in courtship?" My reply is a firm *yes*. A single woman has a right to take the initiative by correspondence, telephone, or personal contact to meet and become acquainted with any person she is interested in knowing better. Of course the approach should be dignified and in good taste.

There are several benefits when women take the initiative. It could mean an end to some long, lonely evenings and weekends. Her initiative would give her a wider selection. It could mean more marriages. Since women tend to look more deeply than just physical attractiveness, they are more likely to find a more compatible mate. Female initiative would tend to produce better marriages.

The courtship role is major in planning marriage and life. Nature and society have thrust upon women the responsibility of child-bearing and much of the responsibility of the home. Surely the woman should have the right to choose a life companion who would be meaningful to her across the years. The concept of women taking the initiative does not overlook the fact that men will continue the initiative in courtship. It does not overlook the fact of male and female differences. Each would still be responsible for the necessary roles the Creator has planned for them. Their courtship should be a cooperative planning process in which both participate and both understand each other and themselves as fully as possible.

But the reader may ask, "What do you mean by initiative? What could a single woman do without appearing too aggressive and indiscreet?" Creative ingenuity plus God can work wonders in solving problems! We suggest the following which may be helpful.

1. Do not live at home with parents too long after reaching adulthood. Somewhere between the ages of twenty-two (the time of college graduation) and twenty-five, young adults may need to move out on their own and cut the apron strings. They must continue to love and honor their parents (Exod. 20:12). They should contact them through visits, telephone calls, and letters. They should ask their advice in major decisions, but they should not depend upon them for financial assistance, for emotional security, or for final authority in decisions. Self-sufficiency and self-reliance are good for both singles and their parents. It should improve a single's opportunity for marriage.

Although most parents are not a hindrance to their single son or daughter's marriage, some are. One single woman, past sixty years of age, said pathetically, "I sacrificed my love life and marriage in order to support my widowed mother (whose health was not too good) and two brothers in their early teens. Now I keep asking myself, 'Was it worth it?' I wonder; they don't seem to appreciate it." Another single woman in her forties wrote, "Being an obedient child, I always tried not to date people my mother didn't approve of. It was not until I was older that I realized she would not have approved of anybody."

2. Do not continue to live in a community where there are few or

no prospects. This can be a major problem for those living in rural areas or small towns. Do not continue in a vocation or a vocational location where there are few or no prospects. A twenty-three-year-old music teacher with her master's degree joined the faculty of a church-related college. She was an excellent musician, an attractive young woman with a charming personality. She loved everybody and everybody loved her. After two years she resigned. The college community was puzzled. Why did she leave? She stated frankly to the college administration and her close friends, "I want to get married, have a home and children. I've been here two years. I am unhappy with the marriage prospects here. I'm moving on in search of other prospects." From her point of view, was it not a wise decision?

3. Early childhood and school acquaintances may provide possible prospects. Suppose Martha associated with many fine boys during her high school and college days. Several of them were close friends. She dated some of them. Earlier in life, absorbed in her plans for a career, she bypassed several fine young men. Now she finds herself past twenty-five and single, with no marriage prospects, yet anxious for marriage, a home, and children. In her quest for marriage, Martha would do well to consider one or more of those former friends back in her home community whom she knows are still single. During the years they may have matured and become responsible citizens in their communities. Also, their concern for marriage has probably increased. We believe it is in order for Martha to contact one or more of them by mail, or in person, and indicate she would like to renew their friendship. Experiences similar to this have worked many times.

4. Single people should avoid associating exclusively with other singles of the same sex. It is easy to form so close a clique of good friends that he/she tends to be defensive, to rationalize singleness, and thus play down the importance of marriage. This type of clique is not conducive to drawing out marriage prospects. This is not to object to close friendships with other singles of the same sex. We recommend close friendships, but one should avoid being excessive or exclusive in such friendships.

5. Those who are concerned about a good marriage should talk it over in confidence with discriminating relatives, close friends, a pastor or a competent Christian marriage counselor. They should not hesitate to let it be known to the right people that they would like to be married. A brother or sister or close friend would normally be willing to keep confidence, and to help one get acquainted with the person of his/her choice. They could plan double or group dates to include the single person. They could plan parties or group meetings that would help one get acquainted with the right person. Many friends and relatives have done so.

6. Unmarried adults should plan to go to places where other singles get together for fellowship. Every religious denomination has planned programs for singles. Almost all large churches have seminars and retreats for their single people. Most denominations have state-wide meetings and national meetings for their singles. One major denomination has two nation-wide meetings for singles on Labor Day weekend: one for the eastern region of the United States at Ridgecrest, North Carolina, and one for the western region of the United States at Glorieta, New Mexico. All these meetings are rich with Christian instruction, inspiration, and worship. They involve periods of fellowship and recreation. They provide opportunities to get acquainted with new friends.

7. Out in society there are many activities where singles work or play. These include talent shows, painting classes, singing clubs, the YMCA, jogging clubs, tennis clubs, racquetball clubs, adult education classes, and so on. Employment at a hospital, a department store or any store in a shopping center or an industry increases opportunities to meet singles. Single people need to come out of isolation and get out where others like themselves tend to congregate.

When at group meetings such as seminars, political meetings, community rallies or conventions, it is in order for you to introduce yourself to a person you would like to meet. You are both at the meeting for the same purpose, say to represent your individual church or profession at the convention. Thus we believe it is in order to seek an appropriate opportunity to introduce yourself. Or, if Mr. Right or Miss Right is in general conversation with a group at the convention, join the group, enter into the conversation, and seek an opportunity to direct some remarks to him or her. Refer to him/her by name.

9. Also, during vacations, Christian singles would do well to plan a program of study where other singles are studying. Many school teachers can take the summer off. Some are allowed sabbaticals. For example, there are many seminaries in the United States. Many single men and women just out of college study there. Some Christian singles could enjoy a summer or a year's study at a seminary and take advantage of the extra plus of meeting new friends. If a Christian single does not feel God leading him/her to get special training for Christian service, he/she could secure employment at or near a seminary, a situation which might open opportunities to meet dedicated Christian prospects. In recent years the number of single men and women at many seminaries is about equal. Not every single who attends a seminary marries, but hundreds do. Other singles have married while attending or working at or near vocational schools (law, music, and so on). It is understood that this decision would be a private personal matter between the individual and God.

10. After college there are fewer opportunities to meet prospects in natural situations. It is expensive to travel, and there may be little time for social activities that would be conducive to meeting marriage prospects. Since older singles have difficulty meeting prospects, and due to the fact that marriage and family life has been on the decline, we feel that it is time for Christian evangelicals to consider providing some type of scientific marriage agency to assist single people in meeting prospects. It would need to be interdenominational and directed by responsible Christian leaders.

Scientific marriage agencies have been accepted and worked successfully in Europe for many years. Only in the past two generations have they begun to be partially accepted in the United States. Now they can be economically feasible. Our research in 1956 and 1981 showed that only approximately one-third of singles approve of the use of scientific marriage agencies. This resistance of singles to help from responsible Christian agencies is a cultural hangover—a taboo or superstition resulting from prohibitions imposed by social usage, prohibitions which rest upon false patriarchal assumptions. If the Christian community would be more approving, we believe more people would favor such agencies. From my experience as a field counselor for Dr. George W. Crane's Scientific Marriage Bureau, I have a gut feeling that when the chips are down, almost all single people who need and long for a good marriage would use a marriage agency—provided the agency was sponsored and promoted by responsible national evangelical leaders who kept all communication in professional confidence.

I heartily approve socio-marriage agencies that are run by responsible Christian people for the purpose of helping singles meet marriage prospects. I recommend *Solo* magazine to readers. It is a quarterly publication of Solo Ministries, Inc. Solo Ministries is an interdenominational evangelical movement working with churches and other Christian organizations to win, build, and bring single adults into a personal relationship with the Lord Jesus Christ. In addition to being a Christian service magazine, *Solo* carries a "New Friends Directory" through which singles can meet other singles, make new friends, and enlarge their circle of acquaintances. Interested people of all ages (never-married, widowed, divorced) should write to *Solo* magazine, P.O. Box 1231, Sisters, OR 97759, to ask for details. Every single can profit by subscribing to *Solo* magazine whether he or she is interested in the personal ads or not. Although they do not carry personal ads, I also recommend *Christian Single* magazine. (See bibliography for the address.)

I am certain that some people will disagree with my viewpoint. That is their prerogative. Of course, young people of college age do not need such an agency when there are dozens of prospects all around. But older singles—the never-married, widows, widowers or divorced—often need, and thousands of them would welcome, anonymous help in finding a marriage partner. Happy marriages are the basic foundation for a stable, moral society. There is nothing unsocial or unchristian about meeting a prospective marriage partner through a social organization that uses the blessing of modern technology. A marriage agency is not trying to play Cupid. It only introduces people. The processes of courtship and all final decisions are made by the persons involved.

It is rather difficult to find an acceptable reason why a responsible Christian marriage agency should not be used by those who would really like to find a good marriage prospect. It is not a violation of a biblical injunction. No person has been mistreated or violated. The motive—a possible Christian marriage—is good. Generally one could expect good results. It would be normal to make it a matter of prayer. It is wise long-range planning for the years ahead. Good marriages are within the will of God, and build socially responsible communities.

Some may answer, "Society has always been critical of 'lonely hearts clubs.'" This is a stereotype! This argument amounts to saying, "We have never done it before." Sound familiar? It is true that there are some swindlers running pseudo-marriage clubs, but do we reject medical science and all hospitals because of a few quack doctors? Modern Christian marriage agencies can be run by responsible people as a non-profit service organization. Others may say, "If it is God's will for people to marry, he will provide someone for them without the aid of computers." This argument sounds strangely familiar. It is much like that of a sick person who says, "If it is God's will for me to get well, he will heal me without the aid of doctors, nurses, medicine, or other scientific diagnostic devices."

Society uses organized agencies to introduce the worker and the employer. Christian denominations use such agencies to introduce churches and pastors. God can accomplish his will both through the use of natural social interaction or through man-made agencies. The process of helping the single person meet a Christian marriage prospect through the use of organized agencies is an idea which is long overdue.

15

How Can I Know I Am in Love?

One fall I went to the woods with my father to cut a tree for winter wood, and he said, "Son, first we must cut away the sprouts from around the tree so we can get at the trunk of the tree without having the sprouts in our way." Before we can effectively discuss the nature of love and how to know we have it, we need to cut away some myths related to the concept of love that have confused thousands of singles, thanks largely to Hollywood, television, the media, and the philosophy of secular humanism. To understand what love is and how to identify it, let us examine some theories about love that are false.

Myth 1: There is a one and only.[28] The idea of a "one and only" in selecting a marriage partner is the belief that some infinite power or force outside of you, such as God or fate, selects in advance a *specific individual* as a marriage partner for you. This one person will have unique personality traits that fit your needs and no one else's. You will be passive in the selection process. You will simply wait patiently until "this power," at the proper time, will present that one unique person to you. When this happens, you will know it, and you should marry that person. It is assumed that this marriage will guarantee marriage happiness and that you could never have marriage happiness with anyone else.

This idea is in direct conflict with biblical theology which assumes both (1) the sovereignty of God (he is all-powerful) and (2) the freedom of man (free—but limited freedom). Man respects the sovereignty of God and God respects the freedom of man. Although these two ideas seem to be contradictory, they are both real and work together beautifully in courtship, marriage, and in all of life's realities. They should be kept in a healthy balance.

Let us illustrate how time, space, and life's individual circumstances are major influences in the selection of a marriage partner. After Tom Ford graduated from the local junior college, his parents agreed that he could go to a senior college. He was free to choose. Tom spent several weeks trying to decide whether to enroll at a Missouri or an Illinois college. Finally, he chose the Missouri college. There Tom went with his roommate to a social group meeting and met a lovely girl. They were attracted to each other. Across the weeks and months they dated; after two years they married. At that point, we may say they were each other's "one and only."

But, let us go back and suppose that Tom had selected the Illinois college. He was free to do so. Following the same process, he could have met another lovely girl, courted, married, and had a happy marriage. Again they would have been each other's "one and only." There are many different colleges Tom could have selected, and at each one were many fine prospects who could have been the "one and only." Thus, we must admit that time, space, and circumstances are major influences in selecting a marriage partner, and that singles are free and active in the process.

The Bible teaches that our wonderful Creator-God, with infinite knowledge, looked forward in "foreknowledge" and knew in advance which college Tom would select and which girl he would choose in marriage (cf. Rom. 8:29; Eph. 1:4; 1 Pet. 1:20). But this infinite knowledge did not make Tom a passive robot. He was free to choose. He actively participated in the choice. Such a balance leaves every single guy and gal *free* and *active*, and therefore *responsible*, in the process of courtship and marriage.

Myth 2: Love at first sight.[29] Many fine married couples claim to have experienced love at first sight. Many singles who claim love at first sight never marry the one they thought they loved at first sight. Such experiences may be labeled "infatuation," or "an emotional response," or just "being in love with the idea of love."

What actually happens in the encounter of a couple who insist they have experienced love at first sight? Let us imagine that one day, by chance, John meets Mary. At first sight they are attracted to each other. He thinks she is beautiful. She thinks he is handsome. They maneuver an introduction. The "stomach butterflies" flutter. They each welcome and pursue conversation with smiles, kindness, and compliments. Soon John calls her for a date. They date regularly and start going steady. Across the weeks and months they find that they have values, goals, ambitions, ideals, and many other things in common. They become engaged and are married.

Do they have a right to insist it was "love at first sight"? Let us go back to the day they first met. Honestly now, what really happened? Was it love at first sight? No! It was largely physical attraction, including sexual magnetism. At first sight, it is normal for singles to be attracted to each other, physically. But to say that this is love is nonsense. In courtship there has to be a "starting place," and a normal starting place is physical attraction. But, at the point of first sight, they know *nothing* about each other except that they are physically attracted. There is no such thing as instant love. It takes time for love to grow.

Myth 3: Infatuation is synonymous with love.[30] No! There is a major difference. Infatuation happens quickly, instantly. It leaps into bloom overnight. Love takes root and grows slowly, one day at a time. *You must be friends before you can be lovers.*

Infatuation is shallow and noisy like frothy water running swiftly over rocks. Love is quiet, peaceful, and serene. Still water runs deep.

The Greek word *eros* means a love which seeks fulfillment through another person. It usually refers to physical desire and sexual love. It is not used in the Bible, but both the Old and New Testaments do recognize erotic love. In the past, there has been much misunderstanding about the relation of these two words.

Some well-meaning Christians have made a sharp distinction between *agape* and *eros*, saying that *agape* is good (spiritual) and *eros* is evil. This definition holds that the physical and the sexual can never be good. Such a concept is based on Greek and Persian philosophy; it is not Christian. The Bible does exalt agape love as central in Christian living, and it condemns the misuse and abuse of sex as being evil. But *nowhere does the Bible place the spiritual and the sexual in separate categories in which each excludes the other*. It recognizes that sexual love is an essential part of the relationship of husband and wife. James Deane says, "Sexual differentiation and the erotic love of husband and wife are an expression of the image of God in which man was created (Gen. 1:27). The marital bond is an expression of both *agape* and *eros*. It is both self-giving and self-fulfillment." This is to say that in courtship love, singles are rightly concerned about sexuality in a potential marriage. This married love includes both sexual self-giving and self-fulfillment.

It is much easier and more accurate to describe love than to define it. Many years ago a single girl wrote Ann Landers asking her to describe the nature of love, and signed her letter "in a fog." Ann Landers replied:

> Dear "In a Fog:"
>
> If you're waiting for your eyes to light up like a pinball machine, don't. It won't happen.
>
> Real love doesn't konk you on the head like a chunk of loose plaster. Love must take root and grow, one day at a time.
>
> Love is association and friendship that has caught fire. It is quiet understanding, solid confidence, sharing, and giving and forgiving. It is loyalty, through good times and bad. It survives dark moods and makes allowances for human frailties. It settles for less than perfection.[31]

How Can I Know I Am in Love?

There is no thermometer, slide rule, or any kind of set formula that singles may use on themselves to decide absolutely that they are in love. A practical answer to the question must be idealistic.

Certain motives, attitudes, feelings, conditions, and circumstances should be present if a person in courtship possesses the love necessary for a good marriage. If you are in love with a person, many of the following conditions should prevail:[32]

1. You will be concerned about your physical appearance (dress and grooming) and your personal conduct in your relationship with the one you love.
2. You will have faith and trust in that person. In true courtship love, a two-way fidelity and trust will be present.
3. You will have no desire to date other people. Those whom you once thought you loved will recede into the background and become insignificant.
4. You will want to see, to meet, and to know this person's parents, brothers, sisters, relatives, and friends. You will be anxious to please them. You will be concerned about the well-being of those near and dear to the one you love.
5. You will delight in the personal accomplishments of the person you love. You will not be jealous or envious of that person's achievements. Of course, if a third party approaches your sweetheart with courtship in mind, you will be jealous. Love is like that! This is a natural, normal jealousy! But you will not be jealous of your lover's characteristics and potentialities. You will delight and rejoice in the accomplishments of the person you love, even though some of these may be superior to your own.
6. You will have respect for the one you love. You will respect that person's beliefs, values, moral standards, rights, and needs. You will respect him/her as a person, a total person. You will be able to work out differences of opinion without quarreling.
7. You will have a feeling of inner security as a result of your love for this person. You will feel self-confident, relaxed, and happy even in the face of personal, social, or financial problems.
8. You will be relaxed and at ease when you are with that person. You will not feel compelled to pose as someone other than your own natural self.
9. You will be lonely when circumstances force you to be sepa-

rated. It will be difficult for you to keep from thinking and dreaming about your sweetheart. You will long for the day and hour when you can be together again.

10. You will sacrifice for the person you love in many different ways. You will enjoy bringing gifts to that person. Love is an outgoing something. It is possible for a person to give without loving, but it is impossible to love without giving! "God so loved the world that he gave. . . ." This is the nature of love!

11. You will hurt when your sweetheart is hurt or criticized. You will rush to his or her defense. This is not a case of "my sweetheart, right or wrong." Love must be guided by Christian values and by rational and intelligent thinking and decisions. But it is the nature of love to automatically respond to the problems and needs of the one loved with empathy and protection.

12. You can honestly say that your interest in this person is not simply in the physical or sexual realm, but rather, your interest is in every aspect of the total person as a complete personality. To be sure, to be in love with a person includes physical attraction and sexual interest in marriage. Such an attraction is a major aspect of love. But if physical attraction is the only interest between a couple, it in itself is not love! It is lust! And certainly the sexual interest must never be the first interest. Sex is a part of true love, but it is the servant of all other personal and personality relationships.

13. You will be proud of this person as the potential father or mother of your children in marriage. You will be happy for your children to have the character, qualities, and attitudes of your sweetheart.

14. Other people will know that you are in love. It is nearly impossible for a person in love to keep it a secret. You will bubble over with happiness. Your relatives and friends will suspect it. They will know it. They will tell you so.

These conditions do not happen in a minute or by blind accident. They are the result of a careful process of intelligent association, thinking, planning, dialogue, prayer, and divine leadership (John 6:38).

In spite of the fact that millions of couples have experienced happy marriages filled with love, some critics insist there is no such thing as love. Many years ago Dr. George W. Crane, professor of psychology at Northwestern University, related the following experience in his nationally syndicated column, "The Worry Clinic."

While attending a meeting of the Rotary Club, Dr. Crane met a young Ph.D. from Harvard who was a new physics professor at Northwestern. He welcomed him and they sat together and visited during the meal. Dr. Crane learned that he was twenty-eight years old and single. They became good friends, often teasing each other about psychology and physics. Dr. Crane frequently kidded his young friend about not being married. He countered with "Oh! You psychologists. You claim to be scientists and you keep talking about love. You know there is no such thing as love!" Dr. Crane replied, "Well, I am confident that love is real and I can prove it to you by using the scientific method, with you as the guinea pig." When the young teacher hesitated, Dr. Crane insisted, "Now you claim to be a scientist, and you say love does not exist. If you refuse to test this idea, then you must not be a true scientist. Give me two weeks to set up the test."

After searching for a potential marriage partner for the young Ph.D., Dr. Crane located an attractive secretary, age twenty-seven and single. She was working on her master's degree. She had progressive ambitions and acceptable values. He laid his plan before her in detail and she agreed to participate in the test. Then he went to the young Ph.D. and described her to him, showing him her picture. The young man had no faith in the plan, but he was interested in meeting the girl, so he reluctantly agreed to cooperate in the test. Dr. Crane said, "Now remember, I am the scientist. You are the guinea pig. You are to take instructions from me." Dr. Crane instructed him to ask her for at least two dates per week for three months. It was understood that she would say yes when he asked her for a date. On dates he was to be thoughtful, kind, and give her compliments, take her some flowers, candy, but not too often. He was not to try to become intimate with her, but to respect her and build up her ego. Dr. Crane had instructed her to be thoughtful, kind, and to give him compliments. She was to see that he was happy and enjoyed every date. Dr. Crane gave him her telephone number and address. Things went well on the test. Both were enjoying the new relationship. Two weeks, then two months passed.

In the meantime, Dr. Crane was making plans. During the third month of the test, an important faculty social occasion was coming up. Each faculty member was required to attend with his/her spouse or a friend. Dr. Crane made arrangements secretly for the girl to attend the occasion with a friend she had formerly dated. This third party agreed, understanding the plans. Since she always said yes, the young Ph.D. did not ask for a date until two days before the event. When he asked her, she explained she had promised before the test started to attend with her former friend, and would not be able to go with him. But she explained, "I am still very much interested in you and the test." It was too late to ask anyone else, so he went stag. According to plans, the girl and her date waited until the young Ph.D. had arrived and was in conversation with others. Then, on the arm of her date, she came in, beautifully dressed, and looking up at him with an adoring smile. When the young Ph.D. saw them, something snapped inside him. He was restless and downcast. Soon he sneaked out and disappeared.

Early the next morning, there was a loud knock at Dr. Crane's door. When Dr. Crane opened the door, there stood the young grim-faced Ph.D. He said seriously, "*O.K., Crane, you win. Now, call that guy off and give me one more chance!*"

What was it that snapped when he saw her on the arm of someone else? Could it be his pseudo-scientific idea that there is no such thing as love?

Yes, there is such a thing as love, skeptics and rebels notwithstanding. Courtship and marriage love have been experienced as a reality by multiplied millions. Love is not achieved through magic or hocus-pocus. It is achieved through prayer, patience, wise decisions, and intelligent, interpersonal relationships. You work to develop love. Once you have it, it may both wax and wane. You can lose it. You can regain it. You have to work hard to keep it. It is not merely sex or an emotion, but it includes both. It is something you do, something you bestow on someone else by sharing, giving, and forgiving.

By carefully studying the motives, attitudes, feelings, conditions, and circumstances related to you and your sweetheart as outlined above, *you as a single can know whether or not you are in love.* You can know with sufficient certainty to follow through in faith and trust with engagement and marriage to experience what God intended male and female to be.

16

To Marry or Not to Marry?

In the beginning of this book we outlined two objectives: (1) to help singles cope with their single life and their sexual needs during singleness and (2) to encourage them to plan toward a good marriage. We have considered the major problems of singles but must confess that it is impossible to solve the problems of all singles in a way that satisfies everyone. We have not meant to judge, criticize, or minimize singleness but have attempted to see it in relationship to God's plan for total life and for marriage. We hope we have been able to challenge singles to face reality concerning both singleness and marriage.

Two men in a Cadillac were driving seventy miles an hour down an interstate highway. They were relaxed, enjoying themselves. After fifteen minutes of such driving, the driver suddenly took his foot off the accelerator, put on the brakes, and said, "Say! Wait a minute! You know what? We are going in the wrong direction!" The other man replied calmly, "Yes, I knew that. But we were making such good time I just hated to interrupt."

Influenced by our secular environment (Jesus called it the "world") many people, I fear, are happily drifting along, selfishly satisfied in our derelict culture. It is becoming more and more common for some to place a halo over singleness and consider marriage as a relic that may gradually pass into the pages of history. I fear many are enjoying the blessings of singleness and neglecting both the facts about marriage and their former secret dreams for a good marriage. "When you meet a fact in the road, face it."

It is a known fact that as single women grow older, there is a shortage of males. There are a few more boys born than girls, but boy babies have a little higher death rate. Thus the number of males and females are about equal during the late teens and early twenties. In the fifties, sixties, and beyond, the shortage becomes more acute. Thus the longer women go without marriage, the less their chances for marriage. For this reason, in Chapter 14 we have tried to help single women see how they can take the initiative to enhance their opportunities for married life.

In planning a possible marriage, you would do well to consider your years of life expectancy. Women now live, on an average, approximately eighty-one years, and men, on an average, approximately seventy-two. By subtracting your age from the average life expectancy, you can determine your present life expectancy. When a woman of forty marries, she has approximately forty years yet to enjoy life. Thus the older singles who marry still have many years to enjoy a good marriage, and they may feel the need for companionship in the later years more than at any other time. In this final chapter, I would like to have a quiet, personal talk with you about your future as related to marriage.

Let us take a brief inventory of your life up to now. Where do you stand in your personal relationship with God? Have you made an unconditional surrender of your life to Christ? This means giving the Lordship of Christ first priority in every phase of your life. Are you presenting yourself a "living sacrifice, holy, acceptable unto God" (Rom. 12:1) in your life style? A person in right standing with God will feel a daily pull in his life style toward being holy as Christ is holy. Are you following the teaching of the Bible or the moral philosophies of our decaying culture? You know the immoral pressures of society are great and that the values in much of our culture are opposite to the values of the kingdom of God. Monogamous marriage is ridiculed by many and chastity is considered contemptible. Traditional values are undermined until many live in a moral vacuum. When one's belief and values are disconnected from Christ, the lights go out, darkness takes over, and confusion prevails. Singles, who move into marriage, and then drift with the culture, tend to drift right on into discord, unhappiness, and the divorce court. To have a successful marriage, you need an anchor. Jesus Christ is the only anchor that can withstand the immoral storms of our culture. The Scriptures are the objective basis for knowing and following the mind of Christ.

Are your past decisions, mistakes, and failures keeping you from considering marriage? Remember, all sexual sins can be forgiven. Fornication and adultery are not unpardonable.

Are you struggling with whether or not marriage is God's will? Let us look at some scriptures which may help determine God's will concerning marriage. For example, "It is not good for man to be alone" (Gen. 2:18), and "Therefore shall a man leave his father and mother, and shall cleave to his wife; and they shall be one flesh" (Gen. 2:24). You need to ask yourself, "Am I trying to determine God's will through prayer, a thorough study of the Scripture, and fellowship with committed Christians, or am I listening to the 'in-philosophy' and the 'in-life style' of our humanistic culture?" Through Bible study, prayer, and fellowship, God's Spirit will be able to deepen the natural impulses of your mind and heart which are in accord with God's will.

Have you always dreamed of marriage? Have you always looked forward to the day when you would be married? If so, your past dreams and ambitions for marriage are a major fact in the road that you should consider in your present journey as you ponder "to marry or not to marry." If you formerly dreamed about marriage but have cooled to the idea or changed your mind, what changed your mind? Was it the feeling that God did not want you to marry, or were you influenced to change by the decaying values of our changing culture? You should consider your vocational, economic, and family circumstances, but remember God's will often rises above circumstances and changes them.

As you think about marriage, beware of the bias of your own will and your selfish ambitions. It would be good to sit down and talk with your pastor or some responsible Christian model and allow him or her to help you think about your future as related to possible marriage.

When all is said and done, it boils down to the fact that *you* must decide what is God's will for you concerning marriage. God does not do everything for you. You must make the decision. It should be a sensible decision. It should be intelligent. God is all-wise and intelligent. If you feel that God has called you for one spiritual purpose only, that is, a single life of sacrificial service in the work of the kingdom of God, then do not marry (Matt. 19:11–12). If you do not feel such a call, but feel that God wants you to sacrificially serve him in marriage and you have always dreamed about it and longed for it, then work toward possible marriage. If you really want to get married but feel frustrated because of seeming lack of prospects, be *patient*. (See Appendix II, "Dreams Still Come True.") If your desire to marry is strong, then it is probably God's will for you to be married eventually, but you must cooperate with him in bringing it to reality. The theology of the Bible calls for a healthy balance between the sovereignty of God and the freedom of man.

To cooperate with God in bringing marriage to reality you should follow similar suggestions of Chapter 14. Take the initiative. Be persistent and determined—saturated with prayer, wisdom, dignity, kindness, and gentleness. At the same time be patient with God. All things are possible with him. In the meantime, while you are waiting, continue in your Christian life, your vocation, your service in your church, your service to others. Be creative. Continue to mature as a Christian, expand your mind, and improve your personality. You are created in God's image. You are not a second-class person. Lift up your head. Stand tall. Give yourself back to our loving God in appreciation for life and salvation.

I can hear someone saying, what about the thousands of women who wanted marriage but it never came, and they lived out their lives in disappointment? In reply, let me say first that one of the saddest things I know is a woman, whether thirty, fifty, or seventy years of age, who wants a Christian marriage and is worthy of marriage, but has no opportunity. So, the above question is in order. Let us examine it. Who is responsible for the fact that many women in our society are left out of marriage? Are we to assume that God is responsible? No! No! God is a God of infinite love and he created women for marriage. The responsibility then, must lie somewhere between the national, social, and political situations that get the sexes off-balance, and the unwise decisions individual singles have made across the years. Our research indicated that 86 percent of single women said they were responsible for their not getting married.

But, someone asks, what about the hundreds of men who never marry? In reply, we cannot blame God since he created them for marriage, nor can we blame the off-balance of the sexes. There is no law in society that keeps men from marriage. There are plenty of prospects and our society grants men considerable freedom in taking the initiative. Thus by the process of elimination, it is clear that the responsibility rests on men themselves. Our research indicates that 89 percent of single men said they were responsible for their own singleness.

What message does the Christian community have for men who never marry? Have these men ever desired marriage? In our research, 78 percent of single men said they would consider marriage for themselves now. Many of those who did not indicate interest in marriage now, were still in their twenties. In fact, our research showed that single men are more anxious about getting married than single women are. When we consider the abundance of female prospects and the strong God-created male sex drive, why do so many single men avoid marriage? There are a number of reasons, including vocation, sick parents, self-centeredness, fear of the responsibility, fears about sex, desire for economic power, insecurity, lack of self-confidence and self-esteem, sexual promiscuity, and so on. Could it be that most men who never marry fully meant to marry in their early life? But, like the tide going out—slowly, silently, and surely, leaving a ship stranded—some single men habitually kept putting marriage off, each year or month giving it a lower priority until it was too late to marry. They were stranded on the beach of singleness with old age, infirmity, and so on. Many such men, in later life, regretted that they continued to let other things cause them to postpone marriage.

This is not to say or imply that men who never marry, and who are not divinely called to special religious vocations, have wasted their lives. No! No! But it is to encourage single men to come to grips with reality, to come face to face with the fact and potential of marriage, and to respond realistically. Young men need to realize that the longer men put off marriage, the more difficult it is for them to decide to marry, even though there are plenty of prospects.

How important is marriage? The personality development of little children rests upon and is determined by good marriages and stable family life. Growing churches and responsible moral life rest upon good marriages and stable family life. A stable community rests upon good marriages and a stable family life. One of the nearest places to heaven on earth is a happy, peaceful, Christian marriage and home.

Singles who desire marriage should lean on the promises of God's Word, such as "Delight thyself also in the Lord; and he shall give thee the desires of thine heart. Commit thy way unto the Lord; trust also in him; and he shall bring it to pass" (Ps. 37:4–5, KJV). While you take the initiative in plans for marriage and continue living a full Christian life in the community, "Rest in the Lord, and wait patiently for him" (Ps. 37:7, KJV).

As I have written, I have tried to be objective in defense of singleness and in defense of marriage. But I have written with deep convictions that marriage is God's plan for what male and female were intended to be.

APPENDICES

Appendix I

Reflections on Singleness

By Donna Davenport

With my wedding day only weeks away, I want to put in writing some of the feelings I experienced as a single before my happiness with Ken Frazier erases the pain I felt as a single.

Recently, much well-intentioned advice has been given to help Christian singles, but even though I tried to follow these suggestions, I still felt frustrated as a single. One of the first remedies classic singles books tell singles is to give oneself to other people and get involved. I have many close friends, a warm family, five intimate girl friends, and about twenty-five acquaintances, and as fulfilling as these relationships are to me, none of them can compare to my relationship with Ken. Lots of people and people-oriented activity cannot substitute for the love relationship between a man and a woman. Fellowship is important, yes, but there is a loneliness that cannot be remedied by friends, family, or Christian brothers and sisters. Just as there is a void left only for Jesus in each of us, so is there a void in us that can only be filled by a husband or a wife.

**Author's note:* Donna and Ken first met each other at our singles' seminar. It was the night of this same afternoon when she prayed at the church in hopeless despair that Ken called Donna for their first date.

The need for love from one person of the opposite sex cannot be satisfied in any other form of loving or giving. Believe me, I tried loving nursing home patients, hospital patients, mentally retarded, children of all ages, deaf children, teen-agers and even V.A. hospital patients. Certainly there was a measure of satisfaction in being able to help them, but nothing can satisfy like giving oneself to a mate.

I am a goal-oriented person. I like to accomplish what I set out to do; however, there are just so many classes you can take to fill your mind, and so many service activities or church offices you can hold, or so many vacations you can take before you begin to get really bored with all the "wonderful opportunities to develop yourself as a single."

Most of the information in Christian seminars and retreats is meant to edify us and cause us to make our relationship with Jesus first and foremost. However, after about three years of attending different retreats and getting spiritual pep talks, I began to think, "It must be a sin for me to want to get married." We are taught to want and seek only Jesus, be satisfied with him alone, and the more you hear this, and each year that you remain a single, you begin to be spiritually warped in your thinking.

I began to think that God gets glory out of my life because I'm single, and if I marry, God would lose the glory. I would lose my ministry, my effectiveness, and my witness to other singles.

I felt guilty about not being satisfied as a single, knowing that as Christians we are to be satisfied. Christians are supposed to have an abundant life. I felt guilty about being a sexual being. I did not know how to handle those thoughts. I felt guilty for even having them, pleading with God to keep me pure not only in body but in mind.

As a Christian, I am not in the world's system, but live and work there. When others in our office started their "sex talks," I would get really busy to avoid participating. Being a 28-year-old virgin is not something to brag about to the world. In their eyes, I am a sexual freak.

So many times I can recall walking into a room full of singles either at a church, Sunday school class, seminar, or fellowship, and looking each one over to see why they were still single. It was easy to see some flaw in each individual's personality or appearance, and although as I got to know them I could see the beauty of their spirit, I still felt that there was something wrong with each of them that kept them from getting married. I began asking myself what is wrong with me; I must be repulsive and my friends and family are just being kind. All the childhood names and taunts began more and more to play in my mind, while I overspent my budget on clothes, makeup, and hairdos to make myself feel pretty.

My problem of being single affected everything in my life—even my relationship to God. I reasoned, "I'm playing by the rules, but I'm still not getting any answer." I did not want to manipulate God so I prayed, "Change me, Lord, make me not want to get married."

Because God did not seem to answer my prayers, I began to think I had not confessed enough or was not holy enough. I became compulsive about being more spiritual in order to obtain my desire—to be married. I wanted all the fine Christian people I knew to put me on their prayer lists because they might be heard before I would.

One Sunday afternoon, I went to the prayer room in our church and fell down on my hands and knees, weeping before the Lord, asking him, "Why did you make me?" I had a good education, good job, nice apartment, my health, pretty clothes, great family, lots of friends, wonderful church home, but I was not living a fulfilling life. The Lord and I have a fairly close relationship—granted I do not *know* him fully, but I have a daily communion with him and a willingness to submit to his Lordship in my life—but I needed a sense of purpose, and I think singles often feel like they are left on the back burner, waiting for their time to give themselves to one person and to start a family.*

In my desperate search for a Christian husband, I put out hundreds of fleeces to ask, "Is this the one?" I often used Scripture out of context to get an answer. I had a habit of making one particular guy in my church or community my "idol." I wanted to please him most, and he was always in my thoughts. Boy, did I get disciplined once for this by the Lord. Ask me how precious the book of Jeremiah is to me now (Jer. 4:1,2)!

Marry good, ole, Christian Joe? Why wait! I'm such a sinner, why should I hold out for what I want? Joe is a Christian and we like each other. I might as well quit this marathon.

How do you, in a sisterly and loving way, tell weird Jim you can't go out Saturday night? And what do you do about Bill who follows you around like a puppy and waits outside the ladies' room until you come out? It seems like I always attracted this kind like a magnet just because I was polite the first time I met them. Books could be written on the unspoken, social undercurrent in every singles group.

The more I think about it, the more I marvel at the wonderful miracle God wrought in bringing Ken into my life.

Appendix II

Dreams Still Come True

by Fern Harrington Miles

As I was growing up, my highest ambition was to be a wife and mother. I was over sixty before that dream came true. On January 3, 1976, when I said "I do" to Herbert J. Miles, I acquired a husband, a son, a daughter-in-law, and two grandchildren, all of whom are precious to me.

What about all those years of waiting? Were these years of misery and frustration? Indeed not. In my early twenties, I discovered the secret of fulfillment is not in either singleness nor marriage but in commitment to God's will. Yet when God called me to be a missionary to China, it was difficult to accept the likelihood of remaining single.

Except for times of political crisis and danger—two wars, three years in a Japanese concentration camp—my thirty-five years in the Orient were filled with joy, peace, and fruitful endeavor. I never felt discriminated against either socially or professionally because I was single. Although singleness is abnormal among Chinese, they felt I had given up marriage for their sakes and respected me for it. I kept so busy that loneliness was rarely a problem. However, I preferred to live with someone else when possible. I needed the give and take of living with another person to keep from becoming rigid and self-centered. Also, someone with whom to share letters, experiences, problems, and mealtimes was emotionally helpful. Being single did not curb my domestic instinct. Gardening, sewing, cooking, home decorating, entertaining were welcome diversions from my work. Being deprived of motherhood didn't bother too much, either. Through contacts with other people's children, I could have some of the joys of motherhood without the responsibility.

I continued to believe marriage was God's creative plan for each man and woman. I felt I could never be what God created me to be without marriage. Yet I had to face reality. Since we live in an imperfect, sinful world, no one, single or married, has an absolutely ideal situation. One's attitude, not circumstances, determines happiness. Contentment was not found by convincing myself I preferred to be single but rather in praising God for providing resources to make each day meaningful. Thus, I accepted singleness like a physical impairment. God's ideal is a whole, healthy, functioning body. Yet many people learn to cope with physical handicaps and have a fruitful, satisfying life. Fortunately, singleness, unlike a physical disability, is not irreversible.

I'm glad I am a woman. And as a woman I have sexual needs, though not for sexual intercourse alone. For sex has many facets—the needs for physical intimacy, companionship, a sense of self-worth, the need to love and be loved, to be self-giving—all of which can be satisfied in a good marriage. As a single person these needs had to be broken down and met in various appropriate ways. As a missionary I had ample opportunities for self-giving. I enjoyed my work and gave it my very best. As a result, achievement produced healthy self-esteem. The feeling of being loved as a child has continued throughout my life. But there was still a deep hunger for some *one* person of the opposite sex to love in a special way. Since I was frank enough to admit my feelings of incompleteness, some people tried to help me. Of the men suggested, the only qualifications I could see were that they were male and available. This was hard on my ego.

I was never able to find a satisfactory way to meet my need for physical intimacy. Sometimes I would have given anything for a loving touch. To be touched or caressed by another woman was repulsive to me. I felt safe only in expressing affection to small children. An older missionary once said, "You'll quit struggling after fifty." Quite the opposite was true. As I grew older my longing for a husband intensified. Nearing retirement, self-pity overwhelmed me at times as I thought of old age *alone* with nothing challenging to do. The chances for a single woman to marry at my age were nil; yet my faith affirmed that "with God nothing shall be impossible" (Luke 1:37). So I dared pray, "Lord, You know my need. You know where the man is who needs me and You know better than I the kind of person I need. You make the choice."

God's answer came "like a bolt out of the blue." In 1975, while on furlough, I received a letter from Herbert J. Miles, Carson-Newman College, Jefferson City, Tennessee. He began, "I have a feeling you will be surprised to receive this letter from me. I'm sure you have heard of the passing of Mrs. Miles and know the deep waters I've been passing through." He went on to say that each time he prayed about whether he should remarry, the name "Fern Harrington" was given him. "Your family background, your Christian character and values, your life of self-sacrificial service, and your lovely personality cause you to tower above all others in my mind." I wept as I read his evaluation of me. A feeling of peace, awe, and wonder swept over me. A warm glow and a deep sense of God's presence filled the room. Dr. and Mrs. Miles had been close friends of my family for over forty years, but I had had little contact with them since I left for China. He had retired from college teaching, was busy writing, and his third book on courtship and marriage was due off the press soon. Marriage counseling and family life conferences filled the rest of his time.

Sleep evaded me that night as I thought of all involved if we should marry. Where would they find someone to take my place at the seminary in Taiwan? How would my aging parents feel if I married? Would a marriage specialist be a marriage risk?

After a month of correspondence, Herbert drove to my home in Missouri for our first date of five eight-hour days. We were amazed at our similarities in personality, life style, moral convictions and Christian beliefs. Convinced that it was God's will, we made a decision to marry.

All my fears proved groundless. God had prepared a Chinese with a graduate degree to take my place in the seminary; my parents were overjoyed; and Herbert's knowledge of marriage problems was a big plus. As a single woman, God had given me a rich, rewarding experience on the mission field, and now the joys of marriage far surpass my fondest dreams. Our love for each other continues to grow day by day and our expressions of love are as romantic as if we were still young. Yes, for those who seek and live in harmony with God's will, dreams still come true.[33]

Notes

1. Some examples are *Sexual Happiness in Marriage,* by Herbert J. Miles (Zondervan, 1967), *Intended for Pleasure,* by Ed Wheat (Revell, 1977), and *The Act of Marriage* by Tim and Beverly LaHaye (Zondervan, 1976).
2. *Your Half of the Apple* by Gini Andrews (Zondervan, 1972), *Single* by Marilyn McGinnis (Revell, 1974), *Old Maid Is a Dirty Word* by Judy Downs Douglass (Campus Crusade for Christ, Inc., 1977), and *Jesus Was a Single Adult* by Bob and June Vetter (David C. Cook, 1978).
3. *Knoxville Journal,* October 24, 1980.
4. *Knoxville Journal,* December 10, 1980.
5. Fern Harrington Miles, "Dreams Still Come True," *Christian Singles,* June 1980, pp. 14–15.
6. For a further discussion of this topic, see *The Zondervan Pictorial Encyclopedia of the Bible,* (Zondervan, Inc., 1975) Grand Rapids, Michigan; Vol. V, pp. 364–367.
7. Derrick Sherwin Bailey, *The Mystery of Love and Marriage* (New York: Harper and Row, 1952), p. 53.
8. Ibid., p. 52.
9. Joanna Magda Polenz, M.D., *In Defense of Marriage* (New York: Gardner Press, Inc., 1981), p. 117.
10. Ibid., p. 157.
11. Cliff Albritton, *Christian Singles,* Nashville, June 1981, p. 2.
12. Tim Stafford, *Campus Life,* May 1975, p. 21.
13. Monthly Vital Statistics Report, U.S. Department of Health, Education, and Welfare, August 13, 1979.

14. Nancy Stahl, syndicated column, date unknown.
15. Polenz, pp. 20–21.
16. For a careful study of these passages, see Richard F. Lovelace, *Homosexuality and the Church* (Old Tappan, New Jersey: Fleming H. Revell Company, 1978), pp. 98–102.
17. Ibid., p. 129.
18. Bennett J Sims, "Sexual Homosexuality," *Christianity Today,* February 24, 1978, pp. 25–26.
19. Lovelace, p. 129.
20. *Christianity Today,* February 13, 1976, p. 43.
21. Robert N. Butler and Myrna I. Lewis, *Sex After Sixty* (New York: Harper and Row, Publishers, 1976), p. 95.
22. Ed and Gaye Wheat, *Intended for Pleasure* (Old Tappan, New Jersey: Fleming H. Revell Company, 1977), p. 76.
23. Herbert J. Miles, *Sexual Understanding Before Marriage* (Grand Rapids, Michigan: Zondervan Publishing House, 1971) pp. 145–146.
24. Charlie W. Shedd, *The Fat Is in Your Head* (Waco, Texas: Word Books, Publishers, 1972), p. 13.
25. *Facts About Obesity,* U.S. Department of Health, Education, and Welfare, Washington, D.C., p. 8.
26. Dr. Franz Halberg of the University of Minnesota's Chronobiology Laboratory monitored the weight of people who ate 2,000 calories a day all in one meal. Since the energy totals were the same for the day, conventional wisdom says the weight changes should be the same, too. Still, subjects who ate the meal as breakfast lost weight, while those who ate the same meal at dinner gained weight (*Organic Gardening,* March 1982, p. 90).
27. Robert T. Levy, M.D., *Exercise and Your Heart* (Washington, D.C.: U.S. Department of Health and Human Service, 1981), pp. 22–40.
28. Myth 1 is a revision of pages 41–43 in my book *The Dating Game* (Zondervan, 1975).
29. Myth 2 is a revision of pages 22–24 of my book *The Dating Game* (Zondervan, 1975).
30. Myth 3 is a paraphrase from an Ann Landers column. Date unknown.

31. A paraphrase of an Ann Landers column. Date unknown.
32. These conditions are a paraphrase of my book *The Dating Game*, pages 20–22 (Zondervan, 1975).
33. First published in *Christian Singles* magazine, June, 1980.

Suggested Reading List

Books

Allbritton, Cliff. *How to Get Married . . . And Stay That Way.* Nashville, Tennessee: Broadman Press, 1982.

Andrews, Gini. *Your Half of the Apple:* God and the Single Girl. Grand Rapids, Michigan: Zondervan Publishing House, 1972.

Bailey, Derrick Sherwin. *The Mystery of Love and Marriage.* New York: Harper and Row, 1952.

Butler, Robert N. and Myrna I. Lewis. *Sex After Sixty.* New York: Harper and Row, 1976.

Cole, W. Douglas. *Singles: Wants Vs. Shoulds.* Nashville: Convention Press, 1980.

Cook, Melva. *Thirty Plus and Single.* Nashville: Convention Press, 1979.

Douglass, Judy Downs. *Old Maid Is a Dirty Word.* Wheaton, Illinois: Tyndale House, 1971.

Hollis, Harry, Jr. *Thank God for Sex.* Nashville: Broadman Press, 1975.

Howell, John C. *Teaching About Sex:* A Christian Approach. Nashville: Broadman Press, 1966.

LaHaye, Tim and Beverly. *The Act of Marriage.* Grand Rapids, Michigan: Zondervan Publishing House, 1976.

McGinnis, Marilyn. *Single.* Old Tappan, New Jersey: Fleming H. Revell and Co., 1974.

Miles, Herbert J. *Sexual Happiness in Marriage*, second revised and enlarged edition. Grand Rapids, Michigan: Zondervan Inc., 1982.

———. *Sexual Understanding Before Marriage*. Grand Rapids, Michigan: Zondervan Publishing House, 1971.

———.*The Dating Game*. Grand Rapids, Michigan: Zondervan Publishing House, 1975.

Piper, Otto A. *The Biblical View of Sex and Marriage*. New York: Charles Scribner's Sons, 1960.

Polenz, Joanna Magda. *In Defense of Marriage*. New York: Gardner Press, Inc., 1981.

Smith, Harold Ivan. *A Part of Me Is Missing*. Irvine, California: Harvest House Publishers, 1978.

Towns, Jim. *My Life: Joy in Being*. Nashville: Convention Press, 1981.

Vetter, Bob and June. *Jesus Was a Single Adult*. Elgin, Illinois: David C. Cook Publishing Co., 1981.

Wheat, Ed, M.D. and Gaye Wheat. *Intended for Pleasure*. Old Tappan, New Jersey: Fleming H. Revell and Co., 1977.

Christian Singles Magazines

Christian Single, Cliff Allbritton, editor. Published monthly by Convention Press, 127 Ninth Avenue, North, Nashville, TN 37234.

Solo Magazine, William Carmichael, editor. Published at P.O. Box 1231, Sisters, Oregon 97759.

Subject Index

Scripture Index